The thing I've always appreciated about Craig is his willingness to be honest when his life doesn't match up with the Scriptures. Too many people are quick to make excuses for themselves and others who call themselves "Christian." Craig challenges us to think deeply, honestly, and fearfully about how our lives may be contradicting our message.

— FRANCIS CHAN, pastor and author, *Crazy Love*

In *The Christian Atheist*, Craig leverages transparency to force the rest of us to take an honest look at the contrast between how we live and what we claim to believe. Craig's vulnerability, coupled with his fresh insights, will move you to begin realigning behavior with beliefs.

— ANDY STANLEY, senior pastor, North Pointe Community Church

Craig Groeschel is a brilliant communicator and a gift to the church worldwide. He has a way of saying the things we are all thinking with an approachable authority that resonates with the ups and downs of our daily walk with God. Craig's genuine heart to see your life's journey flourish, and his honest perspective on personal experiences, will quietly convict your heart and encourage your soul.

— BRIAN HOUSTON, senior pastor, Hillsong Church

Church people always talk about Christians and non-Christians, but nobody ever talks about the people in-between. Most of the men and women I talk to every day fall into that middle ground, the group that believes in God but lives like he's not there, doesn't care, or doesn't matter. In *The Christian Atheist*, Pastor

Craig Groeschel hits this audience head-on, opening up about his own doubts and fears, while setting the table for hundreds of life-changing discussions about who God is and how he operates.

— DAVE RAMSEY

There are too many Christian Atheists in the church today, and through this book, Craig Groeschel challenges the genuineness of faith in the life of the self-proclaimed believer. *The Christian Atheist* will cause you to move from head knowledge to heart knowledge. This is a must-read for every Christian.

— JENTEZEN FRANKLIN, senior pastor, Free Chapel, *New York Times* bestselling author of *Fasting*

Craig's insights and candor combine to make this book a true gift to "atheists" of all kinds!

— BILL HYBELS, senior pastor, Willow Creek Community Church, and chairman of the board, Willow Creek Association

The Christian Atheist will challenge you, push you, and disturb you. It will redefine your sense of purpose and focus as a Christian. Every Christian today needs to read this book. Craig's gut-level honesty is refreshing and will help move you toward a life that is fully devoted to Christ. Too many of us live lives that don't truly reflect who we are as followers of Christ. But the good news is we can change. True Christianity awaits us. And Craig provides a practical prescription for how to get there.

— BRAD LOMENICK, president, Catalyst

theChris**t**ianatheist

Other Books by Craig Groeschel

It: How Churches and Leaders Can Get It and Keep It

Chazown: A Different Way to See Your Life

*Going All the Way: Preparing for a Marriage
That Goes the Distance*

Confessions of a Pastor: Adventures in Dropping the Pose

Believing in God but Living As If He Doesn't Exist

theChris✝ianatheist

CRAIG
GROESCHEL

ZONDERVAN®

ZONDERVAN.com/
AUTHORTRACKER
follow your favorite authors

ZONDERVAN

The Christian Atheist
Copyright © 2010 by Craig Groeschel

This title is also available as a Zondervan ebook. Visit www.zondervan.com/ebooks.

This title is also available in a Zondervan audio edition. Visit www.zondervan.fm.

Requests for information should be addressed to:

Zondervan, *Grand Rapids, Michigan 49530*

Library of Congress Cataloging-in-Publication Data

Groeschel, Craig.
 The Christian atheist : believing in God but living as if he doesn't exist /
Craig Groeschel.
  p. cm.
  ISBN 978-0-310-32789-9 (hardcover, jacketed)
  1. Christian life. I. Title.
BV4501.3.G755 2010
248.2'5 – dc22   2010000140

All Scripture quotations, unless otherwise indicated, are taken from the Holy Bible, *New International Version®, NIV®*. Copyright © 1973, 1978, 1984 by Biblica, Inc.™ Used by permission of Zondervan. All rights reserved worldwide.

Scripture quotations marked NLT are taken from the *Holy Bible, New Living Translation,* copyright © 1996, 2004. Used by permission of Tyndale House Publishers, Inc., Wheaton, Illinois. All rights reserved.

Any Internet addresses (websites, blogs, etc.) and telephone numbers printed in this book are offered as a resource. They are not intended in any way to be or imply an endorsement by Zondervan, nor does Zondervan vouch for the content of these sites and numbers for the life of this book.

Published in association with Winters, King and Associates, Inc.

Cover design: Design Works Group / Tim Green
Interior design: Beth Shagene

Printed in the United States of America

10 11 12 13 14 15 16 • 24 23 22 21 20 19 18 17 16 15 14 13 12 11 10 9 8 7 6 5 4 3

They claim to know God,
but by their actions they deny him.
They are detestable, disobedient
and unfit for doing anything good.

TITUS 1:16

Contents

A Letter
to the Reader

SITTING NEXT TO TOTAL STRANGERS ON AIRPLANES PROVIDES limitless entertainment and surprises — especially if you're a pastor, like I am.

Before some unsuspecting traveler finds out what I do for a living, our exchanges are usually effortless and fun. But as soon as they uncover my profession, the conversation takes a turn. Sometimes our discussion becomes more meaningful, drawing on a common spiritual bond. Other times it grows heated, as the person unloads their doubts, confusion, or spiritual hurts. Sometimes plugged-in headphones and closed eyes leave no doubt that the talk is over.

On a recent trip, I had two flights before reaching my destination. On my first flight, I sat next to Travis, a middle-aged, married father of two, who was headed home from an unsuccessful business trip. On my next flight, I sat next to Michelle, an exceptionally witty and bright twenty-three-year-old grad student starting her summer break. Both were tired. Both were anxious to get home.

And both were atheists — though very different kinds.

Travis was the conventional sort. Like most atheists, he denied the existence of God altogether. He didn't pray, didn't read the Bible, didn't attend church. The only thing he liked about Christianity was poking fun at television preachers. He made himself laugh out loud as he affected a thick, syrupy accent: "I don't believe in GAW-duh!"

During the first part of our flight, we discussed Travis's struggling commercial real estate business. Two years ago he was on top of the world, routinely cutting deals in several markets. Now he couldn't negotiate prices at a yard sale. The weakened economy and a smaller income had forced him to make significant lifestyle changes, but Travis expressed quiet hope that things would return to normal soon.

After openly sharing some of his professional challenges, Travis asked me what kind of business I was in. Sticking with business language, I explained that I'm in the spiritual business — the pastor of a church.

That's when Travis pounced: "So you're a minister?" Doing his best to remain cordial, he asked in an obviously sarcastic tone, "I guess that means you believe in a literal seven-day creation, huh?" Before I could even respond, he began blurting out his rapid anti-Christian barrage. "No disrespect meant, but Christians are the weakest people alive. They use Christianity as a crutch to avoid the real world. And the more vocal they are about their religion, the more hypocritical they are." After several minutes of uninterrupted ranting, Travis snapped out of his tirade. Almost as if to offer a truce, he said, "Well, if there is an eternity, I'm sure you'll be in good shape since you're a pastor, and I'm guessing I'll come out as good as most people."

The rest of our conversation was pleasant. He didn't change my views about God, and I didn't change his. We both hoped the economy would improve soon and parted with a friendly farewell.

Michelle, the young grad student I sat next to on my second flight, is an entirely different kind of atheist — a Christian Atheist.

Christian Atheists are everywhere. They attend Catholic churches, Baptist churches, Pentecostal churches, nondenominational churches, and even churches where the pastor says, "GAW-duh!" when he's preaching. They attend big seminaries, Big Ten universities, and every college in between. They are every age and race and occupation — and some even read their Bibles every day.

Christian Atheists look a lot like Christians, but they live a lot like Travis.

Before our plane took off, Michelle struck up a conversation. Somewhat nervous about flying, she seemed eager to talk, as if our chat might make the flight pass more quickly. After describing her difficulties with balancing her checkbook and handling her divorced parents and her live-in boyfriend — who's scared to death of marriage — she asked me about my life.

Creating a diversion from my "I'm a pastor" answer, I

explained that I am married and have six children. "Six kids?! Don't you know what causes kids?" she joked.

After some more small talk, Michelle asked me what I do for a living. No longer able to dodge the inevitable, I answered, "Well, as a matter of fact, I'm the pastor of a church."

This revelation gave Michelle permission to unleash a stream of Christian words and stories. Dropping the occasional "God told me" and "God is good," she smiled softly as she described how she "gave her life to Jesus" at the age of fifteen at a Christian youth camp. After praying sincerely, she was eager to get back to school to share her faith and live a life of purity and spiritual integrity. Michelle held on to her new belief in God but soon slipped back into her old way of life.

As if in a confessional, Michelle continued pouring out her life's darker details. She looked down as she admitted that she was doing things with her live-in boyfriend that she knew she shouldn't. She told me she wanted to go to church but was simply too busy working and studying. She did pray many nights — mostly that her boyfriend would become a Christian like she was. "If only he believed in Jesus, then he might want to marry me," she said, wiping her tears.

At last, Michelle expressed one final confession: "I know my life doesn't look like a Christian's life should look, but I *do* believe in God."

Welcome to Christian Atheism, where people believe in God but live as if he doesn't exist. As much as I don't want to admit it, I see this kind of atheism in myself. People might assume that a pastor wouldn't struggle with any form of atheism, but I certainly do. Sadly, Christian Atheism is everywhere. There has to be a better way to live.

This book is for anyone courageous enough to admit to their hypocrisy. I hope it pushes you, challenges you, and disturbs you. And if you're honest before God — as I am trying to be — perhaps together we can shed some of our hypocrisy and live a life that truly brings glory to Christ.

A Recovering Christian Atheist

Hi, my name is Craig Groeschel, and I'm a Christian Atheist.

For as long as I can remember, I've believed in God, but I haven't always lived like he exists. Today my Christian Atheism isn't as large of a problem as it once was, but I still struggle with it. Like a recovering alcoholic careful never to take sobriety for granted, I have to take life one day at a time.

You might think it's odd for a pastor to struggle with living like there is no God. However, in my corner of the world, Christian Atheism is a fast-spreading spiritual pandemic which can poison, sicken, and even kill eternally. Yet Christian Atheism is extremely difficult to recognize — especially by those who are infected.

My story illustrates the symptoms. I was born into a "Christian" family. We believed in God and attended church when convenient — and always on Christmas or Easter. And when we did attend, it was always boring. Some older man wearing what looked like a dress would stand at the pulpit for what seemed like forever, talking about stuff that didn't make any sense to me. I remember counting how many times the preacher raised one hand in the air — fifty-three in one sermon may still be the world record.

Even though I never carried a Bible to church, we did own a yellowish-gold Bible that was the size of a small U-haul truck and sat prominently on our living room coffee table. The pictures gave me warm, tingly, spiritual feelings, but the words were an impenetrable web of thees and thous.

Two of my friends' parents always made us pray before meals: "God is great. God is good. Let us thank him for this food." It always bothered me that this prayer didn't rhyme, even though it seemed like it should, and wondered if it bothered God too. At my grandparent's house, we prayed, "Come, Lord Jesus, be our guest, and let this food to us be blessed."

Neither prayer mattered to me, but at least the second one actually rhymed.

Hell No

When I was eight, I attended a backyard vacation Bible school. I was a little nervous, but the games, prizes, stories, and unlimited animal crackers with grape-flavored Kool-Aid won me over. The kids seemed normal enough, except for Alex, who wet his pants twice in one day. (Alex, if you're reading this, you owe me big time for leaving out your last name.)

Turns out it was all a setup for the final day, when the teachers brought the spiritual heat. Like Nolan Ryan's ninety-five-mile-an-hour fastball, they brushed me back from the plate.

"Close your eyes. Bow your heads," said Grownup 1, her tone deadly serious. "I don't want anyone looking around."

She paused dramatically. "If you were to die tonight, do you know for certain that you'd spend eternity in heaven? If you're not sure, please raise your hand."

Still buzzing from dozens of animal crackers, and certainly not certain about my eternal destiny, I raised my right hand.

Suddenly Grownup 2 joined Grownup 1, and they picked me up underneath both arms and carried me to the back of the garage. One escape route was blocked by the garage itself, another was blocked by a chain-link fence, and the grownups' glares completed the triangle.

I was trapped and completely unprepared for what came next.

"If you don't know for sure where you'll spend eternity, then if you die, you'll go to hell."

Hell! Hell? At that moment, hell seemed like the safer option. Looking back, I'm certain these caring adults had nothing but pure intentions, but at the time they scared the animal crackers out of me. Taking my cue from the Little Rascals, I crouched down and darted between Grownup 2's legs, then sprinted faster than Forrest Gump all the way home. Still terrified of that nasty devil and the sulfuric fire he had reserved for kids like me, I barricaded myself in my closet and cried out to God, "Please don't send me to hell!"

Unquestionably, I believed in God. I was certain there was a heaven — although I didn't want to go there anytime soon — and a hell. I'd accidentally burned myself with matches before, so any place filled with fire, smoke, and sulfur was a place I never wanted to go. For years I prayed at night, "God, please don't send me to hell." I'd repeat those words over and over, until finally I could drift off into sleep.

In the morning, occasionally I'd awaken and realize that I'd neglected to sign off to the Judge of my eternal destination — no "amen," no "over and out," no "10-4, good buddy." I'd left God hanging. I didn't know all ten commandments, but I was pretty sure proper prayer protocol had to be one of them. Afraid that I was a sinner in the hands of an angry God, I'd pray, "Amen. Amen. Amen. Amen." Sometimes I'd even multiply them: "Amen times amen times amen times amen."

By the time I entered middle school, I had about forty-seven jillion amens stored up, along with a growing case of spiritual fear and insecurity.

High School Hypocrisy

When I was sixteen, I decided one Sunday morning to go to church by myself. (Okay, perhaps part of it was that I had just gotten my driver's license and gladly drove anywhere — but I sincerely did feel drawn to church.) Pondering what it means to be "right with God," I strolled up the church stairs and sat in the third pew.

Cue another sermon that spoke right past me.

I headed out, disappointed. The pastor had strategically positioned himself at the main exit, shaking people's hands as they left. Seizing my opportunity, I asked him if I could make an appointment to talk to him about God.

That Wednesday after school, I found myself sitting in the pastor's study, which I quickly realized was also the scariest place on earth. I wondered if he could hear my voice trembling as I asked, "How do I know if I've been good enough to get to heaven?"

Although I don't recall everything the pastor said, I remember advice about not being a hell-raiser, not chasing girls, and not drinking beer — in other words, all bad news. All my friends were beer-guzzling, girl-chasing hell-raisers, and while I wasn't their general, I was certainly a lieutenant with legitimate promotion potential.

I left his office determined to stop sinning. It was time to find religion and get myself right with God once and for all. Armed with a new calling, I attacked my next week at school with a spiritual fire for good living.

Then Friday night rolled around.

It wasn't until years later that I discovered Paul's words in Romans 7. He said that the things he wanted to do, he didn't do. And the things he didn't want to do, he did. His story was my story. I wanted to live righteously, but I couldn't seem to get it right for more than five minutes. I believed in God, but I still cheated in school, drank the cheapest beer available, lied about what I did with my girlfriends, and hoped to find the occasional misplaced *Playboy*.

"God, please don't send me to hell. Amen times amen."

My First Great Awakening

When I was a junior in high school, my church youth group voted me to be their president. Apparently the qualifications for office had nothing to do with living like a Christian, and before I knew it, my one-year term "earned" me a partial scholarship to a Christian university. With athletics covering the rest of my room and board, I embarked on what I hoped would become a new, God-pleasing beginning.

I set off with a carload of clothes, Bic pens, my Cindy Crawford poster, and lofty dreams. Instead of being surrounded by young Billy Grahams and Mother Teresas, however, I was bombarded by miniature Lindsay Lohans and Kanye Wests and quickly pulled into the party scene.

Sin is fun — at least for a while. But it never fails to come back to haunt you, usually when you least expect it. Like a sneeze, sin feels good at first, but it leaves a huge mess. By my sophomore year, several of my fraternity brothers got busted for grand larceny, putting our whole fraternity at risk of being kicked off campus. Around the same time, because of a major hangover, I slept through tennis practice, which placed me exactly one mistake away from losing my athletic scholarship. And many people on campus despised me because of how I had treated a few girls.

Feeling lower and lower by the second, I decided to look up toward God — again.

I decided to start a Bible study in our fraternity house. I sold this unusual idea to my frat brothers by explaining that it would be great PR to help our sullied reputation. Truthfully, I wanted to learn about God. Since church hadn't really helped me in that department, I thought I might as well go straight to the Bible to see what I could discover for myself.

On the Tuesday morning before our first Bible study, I was strolling across campus between classes when it dawned on me that I didn't have a Bible. (I left the family's gold Bible at home.) On my way to my world literature class, an older gentleman introduced himself to me, saying he was a Gideon. He asked me if I wanted a free Bible. I wasn't sure what a Gideon was, but as far as I was concerned, he might as well have been one of God's angels.

That night, a handful of us started reading the Bible in a small, sweat-soaked, party-stained room in the Lamba Chi Alpha house. We started reading in Matthew, chapter one, and once we moved past who begat whom, the pace picked up. At the end of our rookie Bible studies, we prayed the only prayers we knew: "God, protect us as we party. God, keep Joe's girlfriend from getting pregnant. God, don't let us get caught cheating on the American history test." They weren't the typical prayers prayed at Baptist student unions, but they were honest.

We were a bunch of guys who believed in God but didn't have a clue who God really is.

Although we didn't know what we were doing, our little

Bible study started to grow. Apparently many of our party friends bore a similar spiritual curiosity. The more Bible we read and the more prayers we prayed, the more people showed up and the more God seemed to do.

After finishing Matthew, we discovered that Mark, Luke, and John had several of the same stories. Three chapters into Acts, we got bored and skipped to Romans. Midway through Romans, I got so excited that I started reading ahead. When I reached Ephesians, I encountered two verses that would forever change my life: "For it is by grace you have been saved, through faith — and this not from yourselves, it is the gift of God — not by works, so that no one can boast." Could this be true? We're saved by God's grace and his grace alone? It's not by our works? Why didn't anyone tell me?

I felt like a caged animal and had to escape that tiny room. Someone was sitting in front of the only door, so I slipped out the closest window and dropped to the ground. Sensing something important, I dashed to a nearby softball field, needing to be alone with God. What happened next is hard to explain and even harder for me to believe. The presence of God became real to me.

I always thought that only wackos actually hear from God. Sure, you heard God. And there's a teeny angel on your shoulder right now telling you what to do next, right?

Well, that evening I became a wacko. Kneeling on the grass, I heard a voice. It wasn't audible — it was actually way too loud to be audible, too present inside me. "Without me, you have nothing. With me, you have everything." I knelt and prayed the shortest, most power-packed, faith-filled prayer of my life.

Not so much whispering as mouthing the words, I said to God, "Take my life."

That was it. I had knelt down in the field as one person, and I stood up as a completely different person. I had the same body, the same voice, and the same mind, but I wasn't the same. I'd later learn that I'd become what the Bible calls a "new creation" (2 Cor. 5:17). The old was gone; the new had come. I had finally transformed from a Christian Atheist into a Christian.

For the first time in my life, I believed in God and began to live like he is real.

Mission Not Accomplished

Since I was a new person, I became aware of a new mission: to spread the gospel into all the earth — starting with my roommate. No one was immune from my infectious faith. Not my fellow athletes, not my fraternity brothers, not my party friends, not my professors. To say I became a fanatic would be an understatement. I started collecting converts to Christianity like Michael Phelps collects gold medals. The more that God did, the more I began to understand that God was calling me to give him my whole life in full-time, vocational ministry.

As if on cue, when I was twenty-three, God opened a door for me to work at a historic downtown church. My dream-come-true slowly turned into a spiritual nightmare. What started out as a good thing quickly became an obsession. My service was never enough. And as my love for ministry burned hotter, my passion for Christ cooled.

My mission had become a job. Instead of studying God's Word out of personal devotion, I studied only to preach. Instead of preaching messages to bring glory to God, I preached to bring people to church. I promised hurting people I would pray for them, but I usually didn't follow through.

At the age of twenty-five, I was a full-time pastor and a part-time follower of Christ.

An Invitation

Does any of this resonate with your experience? Was there a time in your life that you were closer to God than you are today? If you're like me, your spiritual drift didn't happen on purpose. Like a tiny leak in a tire, slowly but surely, your spiritual passion quietly slipped away. Maybe it has just become clear to you. Instead of a fully devoted follower of Christ, you've unintentionally become a full-time mom or full-time student or a full-time bank clerk — and a part-time follower of Christ.

Maybe like so many, you're a member of a church, but you're secretly still ashamed of your past. Perhaps you've heard about the love of God, but you're still not convinced that God totally loves you. Or though you're convinced God exists, your prayer life isn't what you know it should be. Perhaps like many other well-meaning Christians, you know what God wants you to do, but you still do whatever you want. Or you genuinely want to trust God as your provider, but you find it so hard to actually do. Possibly you believe in heaven and hell, but sharing your faith with others is still foreign or simply way too intimidating for you. Or you may believe in God but don't see much need for the church.

I'll be honest with you about my struggles, and I hope you'll be honest as well. And together, with God's help, perhaps we can learn to know and walk with God more intimately.

CHAPTER 1

When You Believe in God but Don't Really Know Him

"CRAIG, YOU OUGHT TO MEET THIS GIRL. SHE'S WEIRD LIKE you. I mean, she's a God fanatic. She's, like, way overboard for God."

"Weird like you" wasn't in my top-ten qualities to look for in a girl, but enough people were telling me about Amy that I had to meet her. I was a senior in college and praying daily to meet someone equally passionate about Christ. From all reports, Amy was everything I had dreamed of and more.

Our relationship began with several phone calls before we finally met in person. Someone told Amy I resembled Tom Cruise. When she opened the door and saw me for the first time, her expectant smile faltered. I guess I don't look exactly like Maverick from *Top Gun*. (But I do have dark hair and a big nose.)

That night we attended a Bible study that Amy led for high-school girls. She was amazing, and all of the love cliches I had heard about over the years happened to me. When she prayed for "her girls," heaven seemed to open. When she sang songs of worship, time stood still. Every time she looked in my direction, I simultaneously praised God and melted. She was funny, loyal, and sincere. Not to mention, on a scale of one to ten, she was a 498 million. (Still is.) I remember thinking, *God, you are good. Nice work.*

Overflowing with anticipation, I was constantly trying to make a good impression, to present my best Craig. I wore my newest shirts, put on extra cologne, cleaned out my car, and created the perfect mix tape (packed with the latest combination of Christian music and 1980s love songs). But more than that, I tried to make sure I was spiritually on my best game, praying constantly to treat her with honor and purity.

Six months after I first met Amy, I proposed to her at church in front of all our loved ones. (Thankfully she said yes; otherwise, it would have been awkward.) Five months later we got married.

That was nineteen years ago, and our marriage is now officially old enough to move out and go to college. During all those years, I've come to know Amy better than I know any other person in the world. If there are forty women in a room all talking at once, I can pick out her voice. If I walk into a crowded lobby, with people all crushed together, my eyes find hers instantly. I know her scent, and a single whiff of it will make me think about her for the rest of the day. I know her favorite color, her favorite song, her favorite meal, which of my shirts she likes best.

Despite how completely we know each other — even after nearly two decades — our intimacy continues to grow. We're constantly learning how to connect and communicate deeply. I can practically read her mind. A situation will arise when she's not there, and I know exactly what Amy would do. I know her values. I know how she processes decisions.

The two of us share a history — stories, experiences, and lots of kids. We love each other. We believe in each other.

In short, we know each other.

Believing versus Knowing

A recent Gallup poll reported that 94 percent of Americans claim to believe in God or a universal spirit. However, a quick glance at Scripture and our culture makes it plainly obvious that nowhere near 94 percent actually know God. I mean, really *know* him — intimately. Belief isn't the same as personal knowledge. For many people, the very idea that you could know God on a relational level seems unlikely, unrealistic, unattainable.

Part of the confusion stems from failure to recognize the different levels of intimacy when it comes to knowing God.

Some of us know God by reputation, as when we hear about a certain girl or guy from a close friend. We may know a bit about God — perhaps we've been to church a few times, we've heard some Bible stories, or we have a favorite Bible verse on a refrigerator magnet. But it's only secondhand.

Some of us know God in our memories. We've truly experienced his goodness, grace, and love in the past. Like when I recently bumped into an old college buddy. Twenty years ago, we were inseparable. We took classes together, played sports together, and met Christ together. After we graduated, we lost touch. I knew him years ago, but I can't say that I know him now.

And some of us know God intimately. Right here, right now.

This is the kind of loving knowledge that God promises when we seek him (see Deut. 4:29; Jer. 29:13; Matt. 7:7 – 8; Acts 17:27). When we are thirsty for God, God will satisfy that longing. And as we continue to seek God, we'll grow to know him more and more intimately. When we hear God's voice, we'll recognize it instantly. We'll talk to God all the time and miss him when circumstances distract us from his presence. We'll build a history together, storing up story after story of shared experiences.

We'll love God. We'll trust God.

We'll know God.

Not Knowing God

Maybe you're thinking, *I believe in God. Isn't that enough? I mean, a lot of people don't believe in God, but I do. Isn't that what he wants from me?* Those are fair questions. But believing in God isn't all he wants from us. The book of James says that even the demons believe in God, and yet they tremble because they know that they're relationally separated from him (James 2:19). Obviously, there is more to the whole Christian thing than just believing in God.

Growing up, my family was what I'd call "cultural Christians." We'd go to church on Christmas and Easter. We'd help a neighbor in need. We'd donate canned goods to food drives. We'd pray at Thanksgiving meals. But that was basically the extent of it. Even though I believed in God, all I knew was *about* him — and very little of that. I didn't *know* him. And because I didn't know him the way best friends or spouses know each other, I lived according to my own rules.

My very actions revealed my lack of intimate knowledge of God. According to 1 John 2:3 – 4, "We know that we have come to know him if we obey his commands. The man who says, 'I know him,' but does not do what he commands is a liar, and the truth is not in him." A little harsh? I prefer to think of it as straightforward and honest. Truthfully spoken by someone who truly cares and wants what's best for us.

We need to keep in mind that God's commands are loving. What God asks his children to do — like pursue justice, love mercy, live humbly (see Mic. 6:8) — is what we want to do anyway, at least in our best moments. We are created to be living examples of God's love to a hurting world.

God cares about how we live. And a relationship with God naturally will flow out in daily attitudes and actions. So if you *look* good, you *are* good, right? Well, maybe not. Knowing God can lead to a positive lifestyle, but the reverse isn't true. Our outward actions alone don't prove that we enjoy an inward relationship with God. Just because we *do* good doesn't mean we know the One who *is* good. Like when I first met Amy, I didn't know her at first, but I was trying to get to know her. If I didn't make any effort, we'd never really know each other. We need to make an effort to get to know God.

God is interested not only in our actions but also in our hearts — in particular, our attitude toward him. Do our good works overflow from knowing him? Or do we live as though God is simply watching and checking our accomplishments off some heavenly to-do list? Did you get a star for going to church? Being nice? Giving money to charity? Some of us try to earn God's acceptance without truly knowing his heart. And after life is over, Jesus will say to such individuals, "You wanted no part of a relationship with me. Go away." (See Matt. 7:21 – 23.)

Countless well-intentioned people believe in God but don't know him personally. Many of us look the part. Or we think we're Christians because, you know, it's not like we're Buddhists.

We believe in God, but our lives don't reflect who he really is.

Not Knowing God Well

Have you ever heard of George Brett, the legendary third baseman who played for the Kansas City Royals? When I was a kid, I collected every George Brett baseball card ever made and knew everything about his career.

In 1988, I played in the NAIA National Tennis

Championship in Kansas City. On a walk downtown, I saw George Brett sitting at an outdoor cafe. I couldn't stop myself — I walked right up to him, extended my hand, and said, "I know this happens to you all the time. I'm so sorry. I just had to tell you, you're the man! In 1980, you batted .390 — you almost batted over .400 — which would have broken Ted Williams' record from back in 1941. You had 118 RBIs in only 117 games. You're the man!" (A bit repetitive, I know, but I was nervous.)

Now, I didn't actually know George Brett, but I knew information about him. And I had heard that he was cocky and rude. What I experienced, however, was quite the opposite.

"You know all that about me?" he asked.

"Oh, I'm just getting started."

"That's amazing. Why don't you sit with us? Let's talk for a few minutes." And he pulled up a chair.

After we had talked for about fifteen minutes, George asked, "So, what brings you to Kansas City?" I told him that I was playing in the big tennis tournament the next day. He congratulated me and said, "You know what? You've watched me all these years. I'll try to come out and watch you play tomorrow."

The next day, I won the National Tennis title ... with George Brett cheering me on from the very front row. (Cue dream scene fade-out and ethereal musical sounds.)

Okay, so that didn't really happen, though it would have been a great ending to this story. The reality is that George didn't show, and I lost in the second round and went home crushed.

Technically, I could say that I know George Brett because of our single encounter. But it's obvious I don't really know him. If you were to remind him about our encounter in Kansas City, he might not remember at all.

Now let's rewind the history tape a couple thousand years. When the apostle Paul wrote his letter to the Galatians (Jesus-followers who lived in the region of Galatia, modern-day Turkey), they had experienced the real, living God but had recently become trapped in legalism. They knew God, but not well enough to avoid getting sucked back into a life based in the law, rather than in love. In Galatians 4:8 – 9, Paul wrote, "Formerly, when you did not know God, you were slaves to those who by nature are not gods. But now that you know God — or rather are known by God — how is it that you are turning back to those weak and miserable principles? Do you wish to be enslaved by them all over again?"

Paul essentially was saying, "You know God, but not well enough to avoid your old habits — the attitudes that hurt you and your closeness to God." In the twenty-first century, we would be wise to ask ourselves, "Is this us too?"

Maybe we "sort of" know God. Maybe sometime in the past we've prayed and asked Jesus to transform our lives. Maybe we have a basic understanding of God. Maybe, once, we genuinely felt close to him. But we don't know him well now.

Knowing God Intimately

Finally, there are those people who know God intimately and serve him with their whole hearts. For me, I know this is happening when I'm becoming increasingly aware of God's presence within me, his provision, his power, and his peace. I don't feel like God's "out there," waiting for me to direct a prayer his way every now and then. It's more like an ongoing conversation: "Hi, God. Hey listen, what do you think of this?" Then I honestly believe God speaks to me through his written Word and by his Spirit.

It's like somehow my spirit is connected to him, and I can hear what he's saying. There's kind of a buzz, a constant conscious awareness that as my day unfolds, God is orchestrating things and sending people into my life. That's doing life with God.

At other times, God may not *feel* as close. But by faith, I know he is with me. No matter what I feel, I hold the assurance that God never leaves me. And he won't leave you.

The psalmist David describes in Psalm 63:1 – 4 his relationship with God. In fact, he says that his experience of knowing the personal God creates a deeper longing for *even more* intimate knowledge of God. Verse 1 begins, "O God, you are my God." You're not somebody else's God, that I've just heard about. You're *my* God.

David continues, "Earnestly I seek you; my soul thirsts for you, my body longs for you, in a dry and weary land where there is no water." In this world, there's nothing that satisfies me. I'm hungry, I eat, and then later I'll be hungry again. Only God can totally satisfy. *I love you so much, God, that I ache for you. I need more of you.*

Have you ever felt that kind of love for someone? When

you're apart, you can't wait to be with them again. When I'm away from Amy, I can't wait to hear her voice again. Imagine that with God.

The psalmist continues, "I have seen you in the sanctuary and beheld your power and your glory." I've seen you. I know you. I recognize you on sight. I know what you're like. Your unbounded might and majesty, the sunburst of your splendor, your beauty — these are greater than anything I could ever imagine or describe.

Verse 3 says, "Because your love is better than life, my lips will glorify you." Better than *life*? He's saying, If I had the choice — either keep God's love and see my mortal body die, or lose his love and live — I would choose to die.

Next verse: "I will praise you as long as I live, and in your name I will lift up my hands." I'll never be the same. I'm so transformed, so overwhelmed by you, I'm unashamed to do anything to express myself to you. I can't keep my hands at my sides. I'm going to reach them out toward you. I'm going to smile. I'm going to throw my head back and bask in your magnificent glory.

It's All in the Name

Most Bible historians agree that David also wrote Psalm 9:10, which says in reference to God, "Those who know your name will trust in you." What do *you* call God? The way you address him or refer to him just might reveal the depth of your intimacy. Or lack of it.

Let me illustrate. What you call me clearly reveals how well you know me — or whether you know me at all. My phone rings. I answer. You're on the other end, and you say, "Good afternoon, Mr. Gress-shuhl. I'd like to talk to you about your phone service."

I can tell one thing right away: You don't know me. You don't even know how to pronounce my name!

Or my wife and I are in a restaurant, and I give the hostess my name while we're waiting for a table. After a few minutes, the hostess calls out, "Grow-SHELL, party of two!" The hostess knows my name and how to pronounce it. But we've just met. We don't know each other.

If you call me "Pastor Craig," chances are you might know a little about me. You know what I do, maybe you've heard me speak, and maybe you're familiar with some of my favorite topics and my up-front personality. But your use of my title doesn't mean that you know me personally.

You might just call me "Craig," and I'd usually assume that you know me even better. My friends call me Craig. We're close.

But if you call me "Groesch," that means we've been friends for a long time. It means we've got stories. (And you've promised not to tell them.) "Groesch" dates us back at least twenty years.

Then there are those who possess exclusive rights to a few specialized, far more intimate forms of address. These are the six beautiful, small people, very dear to me, whom I allow to climb up in my lap. They rub their hands on my face and say things like "You need to shave" and "You're the best" and "Can

I have some candy?" They call me "Daddy." They know me so much better than even those who call me "Groesch." The name reveals the intimacy.

What do you call God? The Big Guy in the Sky? The Man Upstairs? Dear eight-pound, six-ounce Baby Jesus? Then you don't know him. Those titles may be clever or funny, but they certainly aren't intimate.

If you know God, you are likely to be far more specific with him, and the words you use will reflect your accurate understanding of him. Maybe God graciously forgave you for two decades of sins and you gratefully call him "Savior." Perhaps when you pray, you call God "Healer" because he's healed your broken heart. Maybe you call him "Comforter" because he has come alongside and provided company in your misery. Maybe you call him "Fortress" or "Rock" or "Strength." Maybe you've found yourself backed into a corner, with nowhere to turn, creditors calling, and he's "Provider" to you. If you're a woman, and the man in your life abandoned you, you might even call him "Husband." When you feel totally alone, perhaps you call him "Friend." Maybe your earthly father has never been there for you, and to you God is "Father."

What do you call God? Your answer may be a clue to how well you know him. Or don't.

The Best Is Ahead

It's time to be honest with yourself and with God: Do you know him? If so, how well?

If you've acknowledged honestly that you don't know God, I can relate. For too long, I believed in God but didn't know him. Now I do. And knowing him consumes me. Knowing him makes every moment count.

Has God transformed you? Are you different because of him? If not, perhaps you're a Christian Atheist. God loves you and earnestly wants to reveal himself to you. Sadly, our sin separates us from a holy God. In his mercy and grace, God sent his Son, Jesus, to become the perfect sacrifice for the forgiveness of our sins. Jesus, the sinless Son of God, became sin for us on the cross. He is the "lamb of God" who died in our place. Romans 10:13 says, "Everyone who calls on the name of the Lord will be saved." "Everyone" includes you and me.

If you don't know him, you can. If you used to be close, you can be close again. Getting to know God is not difficult, and it isn't about a bunch of rules. Yes, God wants your obedience, but he wants your heart even more. He says over and over again that if you seek him, you will find him (Deut. 4:29; Jer. 29:13; Matt. 7:7 – 8; Acts 17:27). You can find him by reading your Bible; he's been there all along. And when you begin to seek him, you'll find that he's already running toward you, his beloved child. Get to know him and allow his presence to impact every area of your life, every day.

As you get to know him better, you will change. A vibrant and intimate relationship with God will empower you to heal from the hurts from your past, forgive what seems unforgivable, and change what seems unchangeable about yourself. Walking with God will break the power of materialism in your life and lead you to a radically generous life. Instead of living for yourself and for the moment, you'll live for Christ and for eternity. Your heart will begin to break for the reasons and causes that break God's heart. You'll serve him faithfully as part of his bride, the church. Instead of living in torment from worry and fear, you'll learn to experience peace, grace, and trust. As you get to know him, you'll live boldly for him, excitedly sharing your faith with others, less and less concerned about what others think. Knowing him will make you ache to tell others about him.

Get to know God. When you do, you will never be the same.

CHAPTER 2

When You Believe in God but Are Ashamed of Your Past

WHEN I WAS IN THE SECOND GRADE, I HAD A CRUSH ON AN older woman. Missy was my blonde-haired, blue-eyed, and totally mysterious third-grade neighbor. A simple flip of her hair started my heart palpitating. She was the total package. I mean, she could climb trees — and fish for crawdads.

Whenever I was anywhere in Missy's vicinity, I'd freeze up like a North Dakota pond in December.

I tried to win her love the traditional way. *My* friend would pass along a query through *her* friend, wondering if, by some strange twist of fate, I might actually ... um ... like her ... well, did she think she might, you know, maybe, possibly ... like me back? Through the grade-school grapevine, I made it clearly (but subtly) known that, if she wanted to "go with me," I'd probably be willing to "go with her." Whatever that meant.

By day I tracked her every move, and by night I dreamed of

saving her from vicious pirates, but it was all to no avail. She wasn't interested in younger men.

Then it happened. One glorious afternoon Missy asked me to come to her house to see a frog she had caught. I knew by now not to expect any pirates or kissing, but at least I would get to bask in her presence.

Turns out, her presence was far from a basking-type environment. It was downright creepy. Holding Kermit in an old Folgers coffee tin, Missy asked me if I thought she should kill the frog. I wasn't big into frogocide, but when Missy asked, she had that deviant you-really-should-agree-with-me-if-you-want-me-to-sail-on-the-pirate-ship-with-you-forever look. So, blinded by an acute case of puppy love, I agreed that she should kill the frog.

Missy placed the frog on his back. His white stomach faced the heavens, legs kicking desperately, seeking a grip on anything. And I watched as my deranged beauty crushed the frog, using the rough, rusty edges of the coffee can. The helpless hopper's mouth shot open. His eyes bulged out of his head, as he died a long, slow death.

I was never able to look at Missy — or myself — the same way after that. Knowing that my choice cost an innocent frog his life sent me into shame-filled depression. In my second grade mind, I had sinned grievously. From that moment on, my life seemed darker.

Before that twisted encounter, I'd seen myself as a basically good kid. Sure, I'd stolen gum, tattled on my sister, and run in the school hallways. But taking that frog's life crossed some line in the moral sand of the universe. What I did was bad. Really bad. For the first time in my life, I felt shame.

It wouldn't be the last.

Shame was a direct contributor to my years of Christian Atheism, just as it is for many others. When we become consumed with shame about decisions and actions, belief in God can never evolve into a loving relationship. Over time, we accumulate such a long list of sins that we can't understand how God could possibly forgive us. Locked in a prison of shame, many Christian Atheists hate their pasts and themselves in equal measure — and there seems to be no hope of escape.

As a second-grade frog killer, I learned to equate what I did with who I was. Then, every time I sinned in the following years, the lesson was reinforced. I hadn't done something bad; I *was* bad. I honestly believed that if people knew the real me, they wouldn't like me at all. And that went double for God.

Every year I continued to hide behind false confidence, achievements, and superficial relationships. Few people, if any, knew the real me. Before long, I wasn't sure if *I* knew the real me.

It's Always the Shame

As a pastor, I've discovered that many people are dying slowly in a secret tomb of shame. Some are ashamed of their poor financial condition, plagued with guilt about their irresponsible spending and debt. Others are ashamed about sexual sin from their past. Many carry extreme guilt with them into their future relationships. Countless people are crippled by the shame of secret addictions. Some people even live with false guilt after suffering as victims of sexual abuse.

Shame usually follows a pattern — a cycle of self-recrimination and lies that claims life after life. First, we experience an intensely painful event. Second, we believe the lie that our pain and failure is *who we are* — not just something we've done, or had done to us — and we experience shame. And finally, our feelings of shame trap us into thinking that we can never recover — that, in fact, we don't even deserve to.

A few years ago, our church built the website *www .mysecret.tv*, where people could anonymously confess to anything and invite others to pray for them. Many of the gut-wrenchingly honest confessions recorded there illustrate the lies of the shame cycle that hurting people believe.

One girl wrote, "I was raped when I was nine, and for some time I messed around with other boys sexually. I'm ashamed of this and have only told two people about the rape. I know I was just a child, but it still makes me think I'm a horrible person. Because of what I did, I feel dirty and don't think anyone will really love me."

A young man confessed, "I videotaped my little sister undressing. Thank God she caught me the very first time. I got into huge trouble and I'm glad I did. Otherwise, I could have traveled down a very bad path. I've never done anything like that again, but I hate myself for what I did. I feel like I ruined my whole family. My sister hates me. My family hates me. Everyone hates me. I'm a monster."

When our past pain becomes our present identity, the shame cycle has claimed yet another victim. Like a child who repeatedly picks at a scab, many hurt people live a life of unhealed pain.

Finding a Way Out

Please understand that there is a way out of the cycle. It is different for each person, but it is also possible for each person, by the grace of God, no matter how uniquely and irreversibly crippling that person's shame might feel.

When we let shame control our actions, we cannot know God, because we cannot live our lives for him. Christian Atheists may live as if God doesn't exist because, in their cycle of shame, it doesn't seem as if he does.

One of Jesus' disciples, Peter, broke out of his prison of shame, although the struggle was long. Jesus had predicted this fisherman-turned-disciple's betrayal, and Peter immediately and passionately denied that he'd ever turn on Jesus. "I'll stand faithfully by you until the end," he insisted.

Unfortunately, real-life events soon proved Peter wrong. A rooster's crow reminded Peter of his denial, forcing him to face his crushing triple failure.

Yet Peter refused to believe the lie that his betrayal now branded him a traitor. Broken and repentant, Peter cried out to God for forgiveness. After his resurrection, Jesus honored Peter's desperate plea. Jesus' forgiveness and restoration gave Peter a renewed passion, and the courage to preach a daring message at Pentecost and become one of the fathers of the Christian church. His failure — transformed from tragedy into triumph through Peter's repentance and God's forgiveness — became a character-building lesson that led the way to kingdom victory.

Breaking the Shackles of Shame

Like Peter, Christian Atheists can break free from the cycle of shame. We live lives of private defeat, but God wants to renew our hearts and minds and to send us into his world as lights shining in the darkness. Like Peter, we can become convinced of the truth: namely, that *we are not our sins*. And we're also not what others have done to us.

Rather, we are who God says we are: his children. We are forgivable. We are changeable. We are capable. We are moldable. And we are bound by the limitless love of God.

The first step to overcoming shame is to accept that which cannot be changed. In the Old Testament, King David seduced his friend's wife, impregnated her, and used his power to ensure that his friend was killed in battle.

A trusted confidante named Nathan later confronted David about his sin. David must have felt he had every reason to listen to the lies of shame. But instead of giving in to a lifelong spin cycle, he brought his past into the open, hoping to find a way forward. Psalm 51 records the beautiful repentance of a fallen king: "Have mercy on me, O God, according to your unfailing love; according to your great compassion blot out my transgressions. Wash away all my iniquity and cleanse me from my sin.... Create in me a pure heart, O God, and renew a steadfast spirit within me. Do not cast me from your presence or take your Holy Spirit from me. Restore to me the joy of your salvation and grant me a willing spirit, to sustain me" (Ps. 51:1 – 2, 10 – 12).

David didn't try to pretend he was innocent — he was honest. But neither did he allow the guilt trap to rob him — or God — of the joy of a life redeemed and restored. He knew he couldn't change the past, but he hoped he could change the future.

When we hope in what God has promised — *commanded* — our hope is the same as certainty.

Just before surrendering my life to Christ in college, I made a bad decision, one that was all too similar to David's. I was dating a sweet Christian girl, and because I wasn't a Christian, I gave in to a destructive temptation. At the time, I was the president of my fraternity and had a "little brother," a younger fraternity member under my care. He too had a serious girlfriend. One night at a party when he was out of town, his girlfriend made advances toward me. I resisted at first, but after a few more drinks, I betrayed my girlfriend and my little brother. Within a matter of days, our hookup became public knowledge, and I went from being a respected leader to a despised traitor. Life as I knew it was over.

I didn't see how anyone could be salvaged after committing such a betrayal. Yet I feared enough — and dared to hope enough — for my future that I somehow allowed my sin to drive me toward God, rather than farther away from him. By God's grace, instead of turning inward to a prison of shame, I turned upward to the God of healing and hope.

With the help of a wise friend, I realized that although I couldn't undo what I had done, I could do the right things from that point forward. My attempt at restitution started with several genuine apologies. I wasn't surprised to discover that the people I wounded didn't immediately forgive me. But my repentance was the first step in the right direction. And even though my attempts to make amends didn't instantly heal our broken relationships, they did help start the healing of my own inner brokenness. Over time, because of the restoring power of Christ, we became friends again.

For many, it is difficult to accept that the past has passed. Sometimes, it's so hard just to leave it there, where it belongs. But until we do, we cannot make peace with the present or walk into the future with hope.

Changing Your Future

Once we accept the unchangeable past, we must embrace that God can change our future. While we may always remember what happened, we need to believe that we are not what happened. We are who God says we are — new creations (2 Cor. 5:17). When we reject what our shame says about us, we can finally hear what God says about us. He is working in all things to bring about good in our lives because we love God and are called according to his purposes (Rom. 8:28).

Even though Rebecca, a faithful volunteer at our church and the mother of two children, seemed happy, she guarded a dark secret. For years, Rebecca would eat whatever her heart desired, only to secretly retreat to a restroom and regurgitate her meal. Ashamed of her struggles, she somehow managed to keep this sickness hidden from everyone. Assuming her three-year-old wouldn't pick up on what she was doing, she allowed her impressionable daughter to walk in once as she gagged herself. Rebecca never imagined that her child would start to mimic her by sticking her finger down her throat. When the small girl continued, Rebecca realized it was time to come clean about her struggle.

I'll never forget her tears as she confessed to several of us from the church. Rather than turning away from her, everyone — including her husband — quickly embraced her. Rebecca willingly sought help from a Christian counselor and slowly pushed through the darkness of her pain to the healing light of Christ. Thankfully, God has turned this previous struggle into a ministry. Rebecca openly admits to her past challenges and has helped several different women who have lived in the same private darkness.

If you are living with a secret shame, God can do a similar miracle for you. And when he does, we can be even better than new! Once a broken bone heals, it is often strongest at the point of the fracture. In the same way, God can take the shame of past failures and amazingly redirect their outcomes toward your future success. I betrayed my college friends. In fact, I routinely cheated on girlfriends. Deep down I wondered if I could ever be faithful to one woman in marriage. By God's power, he took the shame of my past, forgave me, and made me better than new. My one-time weakness was replaced with an equal and opposite strength. My faithfulness to my wife, in every respect, is an important part of my story. What was previously a deep sense of sin and shame, God used for good.

He's eager to do the same in you.

CHAPTER 3

When You Believe in God but Aren't Sure He Loves You

SEVERAL YEARS AGO, I WAS HAVING LUNCH WITH A MAN
I had just met. For some reason, he opened up to me about his
struggling marriage. When I asked him how God fit into his
marriage, his countenance darkened, and he cut me off: "I don't
believe in God, and I don't want to talk about religion."

Not wanting to push too hard, I respected his stance and
continued to talk about his marriage without mentioning
anything more about God. He interrupted me again, repeating
that he didn't believe in God and that he didn't want me to push
religion on him.

I stopped in puzzlement, then resumed the conversation, all
the more resolved not to mention God. A third time he blurted
out, "I don't want to talk about God. I don't believe in God."

Finally it dawned on me: This hurting man really did want
to talk about God. Since he wouldn't drop the subject, I asked

carefully, "Tell me about this God you don't believe in." He was happy to oblige. He said he didn't believe in a God who was angry, always waiting to catch people doing wrong, and who delighted in sending people to hell.

This time I interrupted: "That's really interesting. I don't believe in that God either."

He looked confused. "But I thought you were a pastor."

Seeing a slightly open door, I explained, "I believe in a good God who takes a personal interest in all of us. My God loved the world so much that he was willing to send his Son, Jesus, to die for us. I believe in a God who loves you more than you could ever imagine."

The man looked at me sadly, obviously carrying a heavy load of spiritual pain. After a moment, he said, "I wish I could believe in that God, like you."

This honest man's words give voice to a reality that many of us experience daily in silence. My whole life I've heard the phrase "God loves you." I've seen it on bumper stickers, heard it in sermons, and listened to it in songs on Christian radio. It's one thing to hear this with our ears, and another to understand it with our hearts.

This is the root of a challenge for many Christian Atheists: belief in God doesn't automatically result in the belief — the genuine heart conviction — that God loves us.

Oddly, our disbelief doesn't necessarily question whether God *can* or *does* love people. We Christian Atheists can easily believe that God loves other people; we just can't comprehend how or why he'd love *us*. We hide our real selves from other people to ensure they won't reject us. How much more we hide from God! *There's just no way God could love someone as undeserving and evil as I am.*

Undeserved Love

When Amy and I were first married, we purchased a tiny home that was built in 1910. Unfortunately, there were only two shoe-box-sized closets in the entire house — enough space to hang a dozen shirts, but no place to hang guests' coats, hide a plunger, or store a bag of dog food. Thankfully, we could store things in the basement, which worked great until our first big rainstorm.

Our realtor neglected to mention that the basement flooded several times a year, which unfortunately we discovered one day when driving home through a torrential rain. It was raining not only cats and dogs but also billy goats and llamas. After about an hour of downpour, we arrived home to find the basement flooded with three feet of water. What few valuables we owned were, to our dismay, trying their best to make like sponges.

I leaped into the torrent and found myself standing waist deep in water. Amy, peering safely from four steps up, helpfully reminded me that the previous owners had left a sump pump in the basement. I remembered seeing it, so I felt around until I found it. And its power cord. (Can you see where this is going?) Looking around for an outlet, I noticed the end of an extension cord dangling from a rafter directly overhead. Standing waist deep in water, one cord in each hand, I had a spark — so to speak — of inspiration: *if I plug this in really, really, really quickly, maybe I won't get shocked.*

I pressed the two metal prongs of the pump cord into the corresponding slits in the extension cord. When they connected, I saw into another dimension.

My body became a pathway for billions and billions of teeny tiny electrons, an open channel for the power currents that coursed through the cords. The piercing shock triggered certain neurons in the language center of my brain, where a long-unused word — a very bad word — was stored. Milliseconds later, the sheer force of the electrical current pushed the foul word toward the front of my face and out of my mouth. I remember looking up to see the horror on my new wife's face. Her preacher-husband had just shouted the mother of all bad words. She also was certain it would be the last thing he ever said.

Obviously, I lived to see another day. And the pump worked. But that moment shocked me in more ways than one. How could the same heart that speaks of the love and glory of Christ utter such filth? And more important, how could God love someone as bad as I was? You might be thinking, *That's nothing!* And you'd be right. I've done so many worse things. But that was in my old life. Now I was a pastor. I was newly married and still trying to prove to myself that I was worthy of Amy's love. And God's.

I felt bad about myself and distant from God because of my sinfulness. Job, the man who lost everything, said, "My ears had heard of you but now my eyes have seen you. Therefore

I despise myself" (Job 42:5 – 6). Have you ever felt like that? The closer I get to God, the more I realize just how bad I am. Even the apostle Paul — who penned two-thirds of the New Testament — had some seriously negative feelings about himself. He wrote, "I am the least of the apostles and do not even deserve to be called an apostle, because I persecuted the church of God" (1 Cor. 15:9). If Paul felt that way, it's no wonder that I've wondered how God could love someone as bad as I am.

It isn't only our sense of guilt that prevents us from believing that God loves us — sometimes it is a simple sense of insignificance.

When Christian Atheists look at the world — famine, drought, epidemics, AIDS, war, poverty, human trafficking, genocide — we wonder why God would love people as insignificant as we are. Six billion people inhabit this planet; how could God love us all? That doesn't seem possible, let alone likely, and surely God has bigger things on his mind.

It turns out that many people in the Bible battled similar feelings of insignificance. When God asked Moses to deliver God's people out of slavery, Moses responded, "Who am I, that I should go to Pharaoh and bring the Israelites out of Egypt?" (Exod. 3:11). King David, who was described as a man after God's own heart, asked that very same question: "But who am I, and who are my people, that we could give anything to you?" (1 Chron. 29:14 NLT). When an angel of the Lord encouraged Gideon to take on the Midianites, he immediately offered his not-so-impressive resume to prove why he wasn't up for the task. The insecure warrior said, "But Lord ... how can I save

Israel? My clan is the weakest in Manasseh, and I am the least in my family" (Judg. 6:15 – 16).

If these stories tell us anything, it's that we're in good company if we've ever felt like we're not good enough or important enough to be loved by God.

I didn't begin to understand how God could love so many people equally until I had more than one child. In 1994, Catie, our first child, was born. From the moment she smiled, Catie had me wrapped around her little finger, the classic daddy's girl. When we found out we were having a second daughter, I remember wondering, "How could we love another as much as the first?" It seemed impossible. Then Mandy was born. She is Catie's opposite in many ways, and yet I found more love in my heart. I love her just as much, but with an individual kind of love. Three years later, Anna was born. Again, I discovered an untapped reservoir of love that I didn't know I had. The same was true with Sam, then later Stephen, and finally with Joy. God gave us six very different children. I love them all equally, but I love them each as individuals.

That's how God loves you. You are one of his children. He's crazy about you. There is nothing you can do to make God love you more. And there is nothing you can do to make God love you less. Love is not something God does. It is who God is. And because of who he is, God loves you. Period.

Love from Above

Christian Atheists believe in God and even believe that God loves people, but always other people, who are less sinful or more important.

To truly overcome this feeling, we must understand who God is. According to 1 John 4:8, God is love. That means God doesn't pick and choose whom he loves — he can't! God is love, and we are loved, every single one of us six billion sinful, undeserving people.

That truth changes everything.

How strange. How contrary to expectation, to all we've grown up believing about ourselves and our God. And it gets even stranger: God loved us first. Before we were even aware of God's existence, God already loved us. Romans 5:8 captures this aggressive love: "God demonstrates his own love for us in this: While we were still sinners, Christ died for us." Think of Psalm 139, where we learn that God loved us in our mothers' wombs. Think of the Prodigal Son, slogging home in shame, only to look up and see his father already running toward him in love (Luke 15:20).

A friend of mine listed all the categories of people God loves, beginning with the letter A. God loves artists, astronauts, and aerospace engineers. He loves accordion players, ankle biters, animal rights activists, airplane pilots. He also loves athletes, acrobats, and accountants — even during tax season. God loves people from Alabama, Alaska, Africa, and Albania.

God loves absent-minded people; awkward people; assertive, authoritarian people; antisocial people; and aggravating people.

How about the B's? God loves babies, babes, boys, bankers, and band leaders. He loves ballerinas, Bible readers, biology teachers, bird watchers, bus drivers — including the bad ones. God loves bookworms, bachelors, botanists, bowlers, baby boomers, and boomerang throwers. He loves beekeepers, BBC watchers, blondes, brunettes, and even people with blue hair.

God also loves bores, the beat up, and the burned out. God loves bosses, braggarts, bag ladies, bartenders, brats, people with braces, Bushmen, and Baptists.

In short, there's nothing we can do to earn God's love. We are already and always loved simply because God made us and he loves each and every one of his creations. There's nothing we can do to get God to love us more, and there's nothing we can do to cause God to love us less.

Covered with Love

If you have ever felt distant from God because of your sin, you're not alone. But don't forget the truth of 1 Peter 4:8: "Love covers over a multitude of sins." No matter what you've done, God's love and forgiveness are bigger than your biggest sin.

When we finally understand that God actually loves us, it changes everything. Being loved opens the doors of our hearts, removing the locks and bolts that were keeping us isolated and alone.

One night during my college days, I watched the doors

of a new friend's heart practically fly off their hinges. Since I previously frequented bars before discovering God's love for me, I decided to return there to share his love with others. I discovered that drunk people actually *like* talking about God. And they all love me. They're always slurring, "I love you, man."

On one particular night, I was drinking water at the bar, talking to a guy who had knocked back a few too many beers. In spite of his inebriation, we were engaged in a truly meaningful spiritual conversation. He asked if we could step outside, so we could talk without having to shout over the music. As we walked out onto the street, we were confronted by a street preacher waving his arms and shouting from the top of a flatbed trailer. *What a good God!* I thought. *He's sent reinforcements.*

Unfortunately, this particular preacher didn't see it that way. He pointed a bony finger directly at me, shouted, "Young man, you are going to hell!" and proceeded to spew condemning words at me. My drunk friend, incensed on my behalf, was having none of that. Filled with the warm glow of alcohol and love, my new buddy leaped onto the trailer, charged God's witness, and placed him firmly in a headlock. That's when my pantherlike reflexes took over. I instinctively jumped into the fight and separated them. (Years of fake karate in front of the mirror finally paid off.)

Like a Roman candle shooting wildly into the air, my distraught drunk friend exploded emotionally in every direction. In some rare combination of anger, hurt, disappointment, and disgust, he gave vent to a suppressed flood of spiritual pain. "See? God doesn't love me. God couldn't love me! I'm not good enough. You're a good guy. If that preacher thinks you're going to hell, then I certainly am. God could never love someone as bad as me!"

I shared his pain. I'd felt it myself only a short time before. I tried to talk him into God's love. I quoted Scripture, told stories, even offered to pray. He resolutely resisted all my efforts. Finally, I felt God prompting me to use a different approach.

"God doesn't love me! I've been way too bad!" he said again through tears.

I nodded in sympathy. "Yeah, you're probably right."

He paused in awkward surprise, a spark of awareness burning through the glaze over his eyes. Visibly taken aback, he shouted, "Huh?!"

I continued, "No, I mean, you're probably right. God loves everyone else, but he probably doesn't love you."

My drunk buddy faltered, "Well ... God might love me!"

Progress. I continued to argue against God's love, and he began to adamantly argue God's case. Right outside the bar, this drunk, broken man convinced himself of God's unconditional love, and he led himself to Christ. (An important disclaimer: this is not a technique that I recommend. If you're a pastor and you tell the congregation that there's no way God could love such a ragtag bunch of sinners, I cannot guarantee such a pleasant outcome.)

God is love, and every one of us is loved every moment of our lives. God's love isn't like the game my sister and her junior high friends would play while thinking of a cute guy they liked. They would pick up a daisy and start pulling off petals. "He loves me. He loves me not. He loves me. He loves me not."

When some of us have a good day at work, we say, "God loves me." If we lose our temper at work, we say, "God loves me not." We helped someone in need. He loves me. We walked by a person in need. He loves me not. We aced the chemistry test. He loves me. We skipped Spanish class to lay out by the pool. He loves me not.

God raises only one-petaled daisies in the garden of his love. (I know. Weird picture. Bear with me.) God loves us because God ... is ... love. That night outside the bar, my friend understood for the first time that even though he'd done countless things wrong, God still loved him.

Love's Appraisal

Not only does God's love cover our bad choices — God's love also makes us significant. Even in a world of so many people and so many problems, each of us is loved by God, and loved in a way that is different — and better — than the way of human love.

Life has trained many of us to think of love as temporary and conditional. It's like the story of a young girl who gave her boyfriend a picture of herself in a frame. On the back of her picture, she wrote him a short note: "I love you more than life itself. I am yours forever. Love always, Ashley." Her unconditional commitment contained this postscript at the bottom: "P.S. If we ever break up, I want this picture back — it's the only one I have."

The concept of temporary love extends into adulthood. Just last week I sat with a couple who had successfully raised three children through college and couldn't figure out how to get along now that they were empty nesters. The wife said lifelessly to me in front of her husband of twenty-eight years, "I just don't love him anymore."

God's love is different. God's love is permanent and unchanging. Jeremiah 31:3 describes it this way: God said, "I have loved you with an everlasting love; I have drawn you with loving-kindness." While others may love you today and abandon you tomorrow, God's love never changes. And because of that, you will always be a valuable, significant individual.

Paul writes in Romans 8:38 – 39, "For I am convinced that neither death nor life, neither angels nor demons, neither the present nor the future, nor any powers, neither height nor depth, nor anything else in all creation, will be able to separate us from the love of God that is in Christ Jesus our Lord." Paul is covering all the bases — nothing can separate us from God's love.

In Luke 15, Jesus was hanging out with tax collectors and sinners, something that greatly offended the self-righteous Pharisees. To help them understand why he would choose to befriend these people, Jesus told them three moving stories that illustrated God's love.

The first story is about a shepherd who had a hundred sheep that he cared for. When one wandered away, the shepherd left the ninety-nine to find the missing one.

The next story is about a widow who had ten valuable coins. When she lost one, she looked everywhere, tearing her house apart until she found it.

The last story is about a father who had two sons. When one son left home, the father waited daily for him to return home.

What unites the stories is that when the searchers found what they had been looking for, they threw parties to celebrate. They told their friends, neighbors, and loved ones, "The one I had lost is now found!"

Guess what? You are that one! God loves you so much that he's searching the wild, dark night to save you. He's moving all his furniture and tearing up the carpet simply to reach you. God is watching every moment of every day, waiting for you to return home, and when you're yet only a dot on the horizon, he'll sprint toward you, his arms flung wide and a joyous grin lighting his face.

Dare to claim the truth of John 3:16 for yourself: "For God so loved [insert your name] that he gave his one and only Son, that whoever believes in him shall not perish but have eternal life."

Why would God love you? Because that's who God is: he's love.

And that makes you who you are: beloved.

CHAPTER 4

When You Believe in God but Not in Prayer

A PASTOR ONCE ASKED HIS CHURCH TO PRAY THAT GOD would shut down a neighborhood bar. The whole church gathered for an evening prayer meeting, pleading with God to rid the neighborhood of the evils of this bar. A few weeks later, lightning struck the bar and it burned to the ground.

Having heard about the church's prayer crusade, the bar owner promptly sued the church. When the court date finally arrived, the bar owner passionately argued that God struck his bar with lightning because of the church members' prayers. The pastor backtracked, brushing off the accusations. He admitted the church prayed, but he also affirmed that no one in his congregation really expected anything to happen.

The judge leaned back in his chair, a mix of amusement and perplexity on his face. Finally he spoke: "I can't believe what I'm hearing. Right in front of me is a bar owner who believes in the power of prayer and a pastor who doesn't."

The truth is some Christian Atheists believe in God, but they don't believe in prayer. They might claim to believe prayer works, but their actions say otherwise. Some rarely pray, and when they do, they don't expect anything to change.

For years, that described me.

Perils of Prayer

My admission might surprise you, since I'm a pastor, but I've never been good at praying. Prayer has always intimidated me, and prayer meetings used to rank just above septic tank maintenance on my list of least favorite responsibilities. I can trace my aversion to prayer meetings all the way back to college. My roommate Todd loved to pray ... and pray ... and pray. For Todd, the longer the prayers, the better.

Several nights a week, Todd would invite people over for his infamously long prayer meetings. Everyone who *really* loved God came, of course, while those who didn't kept their distance. I was caught in the middle: I loved God, but I despised those marathon prayer meetings. Without fail, the faithful would sit cross-legged in a circle and pray. For hours. Sometimes I'd get so bored I'd doze off. (Good thing I had those amens stored up.)

The people who prayed were nice enough, but the whole hand-holding thing drove me crazy. When the petitions and pleas would gain momentum, and the meeting started to heat up, some spiritual warriors displayed their fervor by tightening their grip, tighter — *Amen, Lord!* — and tighter — *Hallelujah!* —

and tighter. Many times it was *my* hand that was getting squeezed, and if I had forgotten to take off my sweet 1980s gold-nugget ring, it would dig into my other fingers and leave nugget-shaped craters. (You'd whine too if you'd gotten the squeeze.) Once when I asked a guy not to squeeze my hand so hard, he reminded me that Jesus suffered for me, so I shouldn't complain.

Hand-squeezers bothered me a lot, but not nearly as much as sweaters. No, I'm not talking about cardigans and pullovers. I mean people who sweat. A lot. There's just something wrong about seeking God while holding a slimy hand that wants to slip out of your grip like a slippery fish.

So you can see why I was never that into prayer. I've always felt insecure praying out loud. I've never thought my prayers were long enough, eloquent enough, or powerful enough. While some people's prayers — like my roommate Todd's prayers — sound fluid and effortless, mine sound more like a first grader praying for a sick hamster. If prayer were a sport and we were picking teams, let's just say I'd be the last guy picked.

Why Pray?

I know I'm not the only one who wasn't into prayer. Many Christian Atheists create long lists of reasons *not* to pray, from feeling we're not good enough at it, to being bored when we do pray; from not wanting to bother God with our small requests, to not thinking our prayers can actually make a difference. While these may seem like giant hurdles we can't get over, we can. I've personally stared each of these prayer obstacles in the face. And one by one, over time, God has changed my heart and my attitude toward prayer. Rather than viewing prayer as a mostly boring, often ineffective ritual, prayer has become the heartbeat of all I do. It can for you too.

If you're not there yet, don't worry. We have to start somewhere. Many of us fear that we aren't good enough, eloquent enough, or passionate enough. Instead of trying and failing, we don't try at all. We forget that God loves the prayers of imperfect people, people who know they've done wrong, who know they are helpless on their own, who reach out to God, who know they need him.

Or sometimes prayer simply bores us. Our minds wander. In the middle of a conversation with the creator of the universe, I sometimes remember that I haven't shaved the back of my neck in over a week or that we're running low on toilet paper. Once I'm bored and distracted, I feel so guilty I don't want to keep praying.

Admittedly, when prayer becomes an empty, meaningless ritual, it *is* boring. But when you remember who you're talking to — when you acknowledge that the God of the universe is honestly, truly excited to hear from you — that truth alone will change your attitude toward prayer. Move the focus from yourself onto God. That's the beginning of making prayer fresh and exciting. *Even fun.* Then prayer is like talking to a close friend with whom you can share your heart, your fears, and your dreams. Then, suddenly, instead of a lifeless one-way conversation, prayer with the Father becomes exhilarating.

One more excuse for avoiding prayer — and this is the deal-breaker for most of us Christian Atheists — is that we just aren't sure our prayers will make a difference. We've tried praying before and nothing seemed to happen. After several failed attempts, praying seems at best ineffective and at worse a waste of time.

But God is moved by your prayers. When you pray and God specifically answers your prayers, you will never be the same again. I know my kids won't after what God did. For years, my kids begged me for a dog. After their cute faces and adorable voices finally wore me down, I agreed that if God wanted us to have a dog, he could show us a good dog that needed a home, and I'd arrange it. That night, all six of my children prayed for the perfect dog. The next day as I arrived at our home in the country, my kids were jumping up and down celebrating. Evidently someone had dumped a puppy nearby, and she had wandered up to our house. God heard the prayers of a few children, about something as small as a puppy. (Which has now grown into a very large and adorable dog that recently ate my patio furniture.)

Pray about whatever is on your mind. When you find out your grandfather has cancer, pray that God would heal him. If your boss drives you crazy, talk to God about her. If you have headaches, tell God when it hurts. If your marriage is in bad shape, ask God to help. If you are considering replacing an older car, ask God for wisdom. Before starting on your term paper, pray for direction.

And if you don't want a puppy, don't let your kids pray.

But even when you don't see the results of your prayers around you, you may still sense God's loving presence as you grow to know him. I've learned that any genuine communication to God may or may not change what God does, but your prayer will often change your heart or perspective. Prayer reminds you that you're not in control and keeps you close to the one who is.

Honest Communication

My best definition for prayer is simple: prayer is communicating with God. This straightforward concept can help put us at ease, especially when we realize that communication involves more than just talking. We communicate through music and body language and sculpting and painting and facial expressions and dancing and writing — even macramé! We each have our favorite modes of communication, and God is fluent in all of them. So if talking isn't your thing, you can still be good at praying.

Whether you pray by talking or by some other mode of communication, God most enjoys the prayer that is natural, direct, and simple. One of the most important qualities of effective communication is gut-level honesty. God hates it when we wear masks to the meeting, when our prayers become showy and inauthentic. Here are Jesus' instructions: "When you pray, do not be like the hypocrites, for they love to pray standing in the synagogues and on the street corners to be seen by men. I tell you the truth, they have received their reward in full.... And when you pray, do not keep on babbling like pagans, for they think they will be heard because of their many words" (Matt. 6:5, 7).

The prayers of godly people recorded in Scripture are examples of straightforward honesty. When they were afraid, they told God about their fears. When they doubted, they doubted out loud in front of God. When they were angry, they let it rip. Under the reign of the evil King Jehoiakim, the nation of Judah was declining rapidly during a time of injustice, immorality, and violence. The prophet Habakkuk was convinced God wasn't doing what he should and cried out, "How long, O LORD, must I call for help, but you do not listen? Or cry out to you, 'Violence!' but you do not save? Why do you make me look at injustice? Why do you tolerate wrong?" (Hab. 1:2 – 3). You could call that a gut-level honest prayer, huh? Habakkuk wasn't the only one to talk honestly with God. Moses, Gideon, and Elijah all questioned God. Job even cursed the day God made him and said, "I loathe my very life; therefore I will give free rein to my complaint and speak out in the bitterness of my soul "(Job 10:1). Jesus never criticized prayers that were honest, only those that were long and showy.

As a parent, I'd much prefer my young children to climb up into my lap and speak honestly. "Daddy, I'm afraid of the dark. Would you help me?" Imagine the same child standing before me, addressing me thus: "Grand Omnipotent Father of the Household, I beseech your presence. Great provider of all I have, grant me thy presence through the long watches of the night, for lingering fears beset me — verily, until dawn's first rays at last light my heart with hope."

Odd picture. But that's exactly how many of us pray to our heavenly Father — or think we have to pray.

Constant Communication

Most of us have a best friend we talk to honestly and openly — and frequently. Would any of us be satisfied speaking with a close friend once every few years? God wants to communicate with us all the time. First Thessalonians 5:17 – 18 tells us to "pray continually ... for this is God's will for you in Christ Jesus." The more time we spend praying, the more we can relate to God in every moment of time. For years I never felt like my prayer times were long enough. Yet God's command to "pray continually" isn't necessarily calling for longer prayers; it's calling for more *frequent* prayers.

Hours of nonstop praying works well for many people. But I'm learning to pray rapid-fire prayers. When I see someone in need, I pray immediately. When I'm making a tough decision, I shoot God a prayer asking for his help. When someone asks me to pray, rather than promising and forgetting, I pray in that moment. The more often we pray, the more our daily lives will be infused with a God-consciousness.

The acronym PUSH has been helpful to me. It stands for "pray until something happens." The persistent widow in Luke 18 kept returning to the judge until he gave her what she requested. When Hannah desired a child more than life itself, she petitioned God continually. First Samuel 1:12 – 13 says, "As she kept on praying to the LORD, Eli observed her mouth. Hannah was praying in her heart, and her lips were moving but her voice was not heard."

Two-Way Communication

All of us desperately need God's guidance, leadership, and affirmation. We need to hear from God. As we increase the frequency of our prayers, and communicating with God becomes part of our everyday lives, we begin to sense that communication is always two-way. Frequent, honest prayers open our hearts and minds to God. In genuine prayer, we relate to God in a *conversation.*

While I certainly believe God can speak audibly, I've never heard his voice in that way, and it isn't what I'm talking about here. God speaks in many ways. He can speak inaudibly by his Spirit to our spirits. He can speak through people, circumstances, nature, and through his written Word.

I once did an interview for a national morning television show, and instead of flying me to New York, they agreed to transmit my interview from a local studio. As they prepared me for the interview, the host placed a small speaker in my ear so I could hear the interviewer. He explained that I should listen carefully for the producer to prompt me. Thirty seconds before going live, I heard a voice counting down the seconds, reminding me to sit up straight and smile for the camera. Even though no one else could hear what I was hearing, the voice was specific and for my benefit.

Sometimes in our prayer times, God's "voice" will bless us similarly. He'll prompt us, guide us, and comfort us. He's speaking. Let's listen.

Unanswered Prayer

If good prayer is so simple, why doesn't God seem to answer more prayers?

Some might respond that God answers all prayers. He just doesn't always say yes. For years, I prayed for the chance to meet one of my heroes, Billy Graham. Many of my friends have met him. I've even been in the same place as Reverend Graham on two occasions. Yet we've never met. I've wondered, was my request too small for God? Did I have the wrong motives? Did God want to teach me something by saying no?

Years ago I saw a curious young girl named Erin walking straight toward a fan with her pointer finger aimed directly at the spinning blades. Although the fan had a protective grating, someone had cut a four-inch hole in the plastic cover, creating more than enough space for Erin's inquisitive finger. Instinctively I jumped to block her. She glared at me, like I was the cruelest person who'd ever lived. I kept her from getting what she wanted, because what she wanted would have hurt her.

Too often we act like Erin. We believe that what we *want*

is what we *need*. And if God doesn't hop to it and meet our whims, we cry like babies.

An unanswered prayer reminds me that prayer isn't a magic formula where we do X and Y and God is obligated to do Z. Prayer is, instead, a mysterious conversation with God.

Even though we'll never fully understand why God answers yes to some prayers and says no to others, Scripture shows us several things that matter when we pray. If we're not following God in these important ways, it will limit our effectiveness when petitioning God.

First, in situations of unanswered prayer, many of us need to give thought to our relationships with other people. In Mark 11:24, Jesus said, "Therefore I tell you, whatever you ask for in prayer, believe that you have received it, and it will be yours." That is an over-the-top amazing promise! But many people forget to keep reading. Verse 25 says, "And when you stand praying, if you hold anything against anyone, forgive him, so that your Father in heaven may forgive you your sins." How can we say we love God if we harbor unforgiveness and hatred toward someone else?

Not only do your relationships matter, so do your motives. James 4:3 says, "When you ask, you do not receive, because you ask with wrong motives." Praying with impure motives has been a common problem throughout history. During Jesus' time on earth, the Pharisees often prayed long and loud prayers on the street corners to be seen by people. They wanted everyone to believe they were spiritual, but their prayers were really just a performance.

It is not uncommon for people to pray with selfish motives today, and such selfish praying is easy to fall into. How many people do you think pray to win the same lottery, promising to give a portion to the church? *God, if you help me win a million bucks, I'll be sure you get your cut.* It's amazing to me how self-centered our prayers can be, especially when it comes to our standard of living. For example, some Christians in the United States are praying for economic recovery (which isn't wrong) while Christians in other parts of the world are praying for enough to eat. Some pray for their favorite sports team to win, all the while forgetting that someone on the other side might be praying for the same thing. We're tempted to believe that if our desire might make us happy, then it must be a good prayer. I recently met a guy who was praying daily for a cute girl to become a Christian so he could make the moves on her. I wondered if he really cared about her, or just her looks and the prestige he'd feel. Only God knows his motives. "All a man's ways seem innocent to him, but motives are weighed by the LORD" (Prov. 16:2).

The way we live also matters when we pray. Although we're made right with God by faith, and not by works, the effectiveness of our prayers is often tied to the holiness of our lives. James 5:16 says, "The prayer of a righteous man is powerful and effective." Psalm 34:15 also tells us, "The eyes of the LORD are on the righteous and his ears are attentive to their cry."

This doesn't mean that if you're mostly righteous, God must do everything you ask him to do exactly as you say. It also doesn't mean that if you are a total mess, God will never answer your prayers. It means that the way we live is one factor that makes a difference.

Another ingredient of effective prayer is our faith. James 1:6 – 7 says, "But when he asks, he must believe and not doubt, because he who doubts is like a wave of the sea, blown and tossed by the wind. That man should not think he will receive anything from the Lord." God responds to our faith.

When my oldest daughter was young, she contracted a bad case of poison ivy. The doctor gave us a medicated cream for it, but he advised us that it might be better just to wait it out. Catie, full of childlike faith, agreed: "Don't worry. I've already asked Jesus to heal me." I was afraid she might be too young for her first lesson in unanswered prayer, so I tried to cool her red-hot faith.

The next morning, she ran into our bedroom buck naked. With her arms in the air, signaling victory, she screamed, "Taaa daaa!" Her skin blemishes had vanished — God honored her childlike faith.

Of course, no matter how strong our relationships, no matter how pure our motives, no matter how we live or how much faith we possess, if we ask something contrary to God's will, God, in his mercy, won't give us what we want. First John 5:14 – 15 says, "This is the confidence we have in approaching God: that if we ask anything *according to his will*, he hears us. And if we know that he hears us — whatever we ask — we know that we have what we asked of him" (emphasis mine). Some believe we can name things and claim things — or blab them and grab them, as I like to say. But we can't. God will give us only what is according to his will, and his will might not be that we get a new SUV every two years.

If anyone should have had his prayers answered, it was the apostle Paul. Yet he prayed three times that God would remove from him the thorn in his side. Instead of acquiescing, God told Paul in 2 Corinthians 12:9, "My grace is sufficient for you, for my power is made perfect in weakness." Though Paul may not have understood or even liked God's response, God had a purpose. Through Paul's struggle, he learned to embrace his situation and depend on God in a way he'd never had to before.

Unanswered prayers can be frustrating, especially when you're almost certain that what you're praying for must be God's will. In such times, I try to remember that God's will often differs from mine. And his is the one that matters most.

Answered Prayer

Few things are more powerful than watching God answer our prayers. I'm often amazed at God's unexpected creativity in his answers, answers that can be far different from what we think they should be. Three years after we started Life Church, we had successfully built our first building, only to realize a few months later that it was far too small. Even with two services on Saturday and four on Sunday, we were still turning people away. The leadership of our young church devoted time to fasting and prayer, asking God to help us raise enough money to build a larger facility. After months of praying, we launched a major three-year fundraiser that fell pitifully short of our need.

As I reflected on God's faithfulness, it seemed odd that he'd miraculously give me a new puppy, but shun our request for a building with which to share the good news with more people. Why wouldn't God do what we needed him to do? Embarrassed, we called off our expansion project. I was deeply confused. Didn't God want us to reach more people?

One day in a staff meeting, someone raised a new idea. "What if we had church at another location?" To this day, none of us can remember whose idea it was. But we decided to chase it down. Within a month, we were holding services both at our normal building and seven miles away at a theater. Suddenly, without any planning, we'd become one church in two locations, which has enabled us to reach far more people than with a single location. Looking back, I realized that God answered our prayers — just not in the way I expected.

You might experience similar results — God answering your prayer in an unexpected way — from your prayer time. Friends of ours prayed for years that God would bless them with children. Year after year they were brokenhearted, still unable to conceive. When they heard about a teenage girl who'd just given birth but was unwilling to care for her infant son, this couple inquired about adopting the child. Less than a year after taking the baby in as a foster child, the adoption was finalized. One adoption led to three more, and the family praised God for his answer to their prayer. God never gave them children by natural birth, but he revealed to them even more about his love through the honor of adopting children into their family.

The Beauty and Mystery of Prayer

Many Christian Atheists believe in God but don't practice regular prayer, believing they aren't good enough, don't know how to pray, or that God won't answer their prayers. Yet the truth is this: the God of the universe is ready to hear from you. Perhaps it's time to call on him, and to listen to his answer.

God will answer some prayers the way you want, and others he won't. That's the mystery of prayer. Even though we can't reduce prayer to a formula, we are instructed to pray honestly, openly, and continually. Part of our prayer lives will be not only talking to God but also listening for his voice. We communicate with our God who is always present, always listening, and always caring — and the One who does all this is love.

Why not start praying now? Talk to God about whatever is on your heart. Cry to him if you need to. If you're hurting, unload on him like Habakkuk did. He can handle it. If you feel alone, ask him to comfort you with his presence. If you've been away for a while, tell him you're ready to come home. If you're angry, let it rip.

If you're a Christian Atheist who rarely prays, it is my prayer for you that you would, together with other Christians, discover how wide and long and high and deep is the love of God, the God who is able to do immeasurably more than all we ask or imagine.

CHAPTER 5

When You Believe in God but Don't Think He's Fair

For more than six years, Michael and Andrea dreamed of conceiving a baby. After several heartbreaks, finally, they found a reason to celebrate: They had made it through that crucial first trimester! They began looking forward to the birth of a healthy baby girl.

Suddenly, at the beginning of her third trimester, Andrea started contracting prematurely, so her doctors sentenced her to two months of bed rest. Even after all of their careful intervention, Andrea gave birth to a three-pound, two-ounce baby girl. Emily Grace lived almost forty-eight hours.

When I walked into their hospital room, Michael and Andrea were cuddling their lifeless infant together. As a dad, I immediately felt their devastation. My mind raced, looking for words that might comfort them. Andrea turned to me and broke the haunting silence with a whisper. "Please don't tell me my baby died for a reason."

No one said anything for the next half hour. We just held each other and cried. No explanation could have softened this family's grief.

People often say, "Life isn't fair." That's unquestionably true. And when unexplained tragedies like Michael and Andrea's invade our lives, even those of us who believe in God may want to scream, "God's not fair!" If God *is* fair, then why do the unrighteous seem to prosper so often, even as the faithful are suffering? If God's fair, why doesn't he do something about all the injustices in the world? It seems reasonable, then, to conclude that either God isn't fair, or he's powerless.

Either way, the Christian Atheist lives as though God doesn't exist. Since many Christian Atheists struggle with believing God answers prayers, it's only logical to conclude that God isn't making a lot of difference in the world anyway.

The last few weeks at my church have been really rough, as I've witnessed suffering that seems outright unjust. An innocent husband discovered that his wife had had a two-year affair — with his best friend. A godly woman lost her husband to cancer, and now she's struggling to raise their three children, all under the age of five. A young girl revealed that her father had sexually molested her for years — and he was a pastor. A couple's seventeen-year-old son fell asleep while he was driving; he died instantly when his car struck a tree. Two parents lost their baby to drowning in a neighbor's pool.

All of that happened in one church in one town in less than one month. Where is God in that kind of pain?

Pain, Pain, Go Away

Unanswered pain spills all over the pages of the Bible too. Consider Job's story.

Satan once challenged God: "Say, God, you put on a good show, but bottom line: no one really loves you. And no one really fears you" (my paraphrase).

God answered by presenting Exhibit A, one of his star servants, Job: "Then the LORD said to Satan, 'Have you considered my servant Job? There is no one on earth like him; he is blameless and upright, a man who fears God and shuns evil'" (Job 1:8).

But Satan argued back: "Hey, no fair! He doesn't count. You've gone and put a Fort Knox – strength hedge around that man. No wonder he's such a goody-goody! You never let anything happen to rattle his safe little life."

God was ready for Satan's objection. He knew his man Job better than Job knew himself. He came right back at Satan: "Go ahead. Do your worst. Do whatever you want in Job's world. Just don't harm the man himself."

Now, if you're keeping score, that means almost everything of value in Job's life was fair game: his house, his lucrative livestock business, and everything else he owned. Even his kids! And as the story goes, Satan took full advantage of the latitude God had granted him. He devastated Job.

I don't know about you, but that bothers me. Why would God allow someone who's been faithful for years to lose

everything but his life, just to settle some cosmic argument?
That hardly seems fair.

In the New Testament, God empowered John the Baptist to
prepare the way for Jesus. Despite the occasional idiosyncrasy
(like his taste for locust appetizers), John was morally upright
in every way. God even chose him to baptize Jesus in the Jordan
River. No one showed the Messiah more honor than John the
Baptist. And yet when King Herod's stepdaughter, at the urging
of her mother, Herodias, begged for John's head on a platter,
God did nothing to protect his son's loyal follower. John was
beheaded. (See Matt. 11:1 – 6; 14:1 – 12.)

Consider even Jesus himself. In Matthew 27, we find him
standing before Pontius Pilate, who found himself in a bind.
He had the authority to release one of two prisoners. He could
release Jesus, a great teacher and spiritual leader who had
healed the sick, raised the dead, and loved the outcasts. And
who Pilate knew was innocent. Or he could release Barabbas,
a notorious murderous revolutionary. Pilate took the coward's
way out. He turned a legal proceeding into a popularity contest
and allowed the crowd to make what should have been his
decision. The crowd chose Barabbas.

The guilty man was set free. The innocent man was
condemned.

Why doesn't God seem fair? As you try to process the pain
in your life and in the lives of those around you, you might
find yourself asking that same question. Maybe you prayed for
something to get better, but it only got worse. Maybe you're
suffering because of someone else's sinful actions. Maybe you've

raised your child as best you could, but your child is drifting farther and farther from God. Maybe you've lived morally and begged God for a spouse, but you're still alone. Maybe you've done everything you know to do, but it feels like life suckerpunched you, and now it's kicking you while you're down. Maybe you've been looking for a reason behind your suffering, and it's beginning to take a toll on your faith.

Where is God when life's not fair?

Present in the Pain

When we've been hurt, let down, deeply disappointed, we wonder if God is there. And if he *is* there, does he even care? And if he cares, why doesn't he do anything about it? God understands when we ask these questions.

When we're hurting and confused, we need to remember a few truths about God. First, God cares for each one of us. When we hurt, he hurts. Remember: God was a man for a time, so he knows *exactly* how we feel. Matthew 9:36 tells us about Jesus' deep compassion for people in emotional pain, a people who were "harassed and helpless." The Greek word for compassion, *splagchnizomai* (splahnk-NEE-zaw-my), means "to feel deeply, as from deep within one's bowels." Jesus felt the pain of those people deep down in his gut. We might say "in his bones," "in his heart of hearts," or "in his core."

And God already felt that way before he sent Jesus to us. God describes himself to Moses in Exodus 34:6 as "the LORD, the LORD, the *compassionate* and gracious God, slow to anger, abounding in love and faithfulness" (emphasis mine). The part of his name that translates into our word "compassionate" is the Hebrew word *rachuwm* (rakh-OOM), which is derived from the same origin as the Hebrew word for "womb." God's compassion comes from deep within his very core. It's the same as Jesus' compassion.

When you hurt, he hurts.

My youngest daughter was recently injured in a bloody accident. (I promise I'll tell you the whole story in a later chapter.) When I rushed her to the emergency room, although I wasn't physically experiencing the same pain she was feeling, I certainly shared that pain with her. I was hurting in a way that only a parent can. When the lady at the admissions desk asked me my daughter's full name, I was so distraught that I could only remember her nickname: JoJo. The woman looked over her glasses at me, raised one eyebrow, and frowned for a moment. Then she went back to pecking at her computer, presumably putting in "JoJo."

"And what is ... little *JoJo's* birthday?" she asked, trying to be accommodating.

"It's ... It's ... No, wait. It's ..." I stammered.

I simply couldn't draw it to the front of my mind. It was in there somewhere, but JoJo's suffering simply overwhelmed my cognitive abilities. Thankfully, even though God feels our pain, he is still able to think. Because of what his Son endured on the cross, when we face any kind of pain, he knows how we feel.

Another truth about God is that he comforts us in our pain. Isaiah 49:13 says, "For the LORD comforts his people and will have compassion on his afflicted ones." Often, just knowing that he's there is comforting.

A close friend of mine died tragically when he was just thirty-two, an event that sent my world spinning. He was too young. He still had so much life in him. Because I was both his friend and his pastor, his family asked me to perform his funeral. Of course, I knew I had to. I sat in my living room, barely able to breathe. What would I say? How was I going to hold it together? He was my friend too. When was I going to grieve? I remember staring blankly at the wall, wondering, *Who ministers to the minister?* I felt selfish, but I just couldn't shake my pain. In that same moment, there was a knock at the door. When I opened the door, there stood four couples from our small-group Bible study. They said hello, led me into my living room, and all of them took turns putting their arms around me and praying for me as I sobbed loudly. I don't remember anything any of them said, not a single word. But just having them with me through my grief made all the difference in the world. Simply the presence of a loved one is often the most comforting thing. And there is no better loved one than God, present in his children.

Thankfully, God is present with us always — but especially in our pain. The Psalms are full of King David's crying out to God — our deliverer, our shield, our strong tower — in moments of desperation. God wants us to be always aware of his presence and to find comfort in his concern, his involvement, and his presence.

Sometimes God may intervene to prevent or ease our

pain, or even to help us escape from it. But we may not always recognize his loving action when it happens. We can't count how many times our gracious Father has protected us from certain harm because we don't know it even took place. And even when we do see instances when he protected us, we may find it hard to recall those moments when we face a season of pain. Fresh pain can consume us, enshrouding our whole world like a deep fog. A single moment of pain can stretch out, feeling like it's spilling over the borders of the present into both the past and the future. But when we're ready, a gentle reminder of God's previous (and continuing) goodness can comfort and inspire us to find hope again.

Near the end of her life, when my grandmother was seventy-eight years old, she still lived by herself. One Friday afternoon, a stroke overtook her as she walked into her bathroom. (When I remember this tragedy, I just ache for her.) Suffering immensely, Grandma, my hero, lay alone, paralyzed, a prisoner on her own bathroom floor. She was there for three agonizing days, alone. No one knew she was hurt. No one came for her.

Finally, on Monday morning, one of Grandma's neighbors decided to check up on her. When no one came to the door for several minutes, the neighbor called for help. Police and an ambulance arrived shortly, and they broke in and found her. The paramedics whisked Grandma to the emergency room, giving her the first relief she'd felt in seventy-two long hours.

I'd love to tell you why God allowed my grandma to suffer alone on the cold hard bathroom floor, but I can't. I'd love to say it was all part of God's plan and that he used it in big ways. Again, I can't. I wish I could tell you that Grandma shared her faith with a nurse in the hospital, who then began to follow Christ. I wish I could tell you Grandma was healed that day and that she fully recovered. I can't tell you any of those things. The truth is, Grandma never recovered. She spent her remaining six months on this earth partially paralyzed, under the constant care of physicians.

Before Grandma died, I asked her what she thought about when she was alone on the floor. I'll never forget what she said: "I've never been closer to God my whole life than when I was in pain."

God Is Not Fair

God is not a finite person. He is a spirit who created everything. He doesn't experience time the way that we do. We cannot realistically expect to fully understand God's perspective, especially when it comes to pain and suffering. However, we can examine what we know about God and what we know about ourselves. If you're like me, when something bad happens, you often feel like your pain is unjustified. *It's just not fair. I'm a good person. I didn't do anything to deserve this.* There is one major problem with my defense: I'm not good.

But the good news is that God is not fair. Psalm 103:10 – 12 says, "[God] does not treat us as our sins deserve or repay us according to our iniquities. For as high as the heavens are above the earth, so great is his love for those who fear him;

as far as the east is from the west, so far has he removed our transgressions from us." If the wages of sin is death and we're sinners, then we deserve death. We've broken the law. We're guilty. We deserve to be punished. To die and suffer eternally would be fair punishment for our disobedience. But thank God, he's not fair.

He is *just*, but he is not fair.

Because someone sinned, someone must die. In his mercy, God sent his Son, Jesus, as a sacrifice for our sins. If we know Jesus, he doesn't give us what we deserve. We read earlier in Romans 6:23, "The wages of sin is death." That's what we deserve. But that verse doesn't end there. It continues, "But the gift of God is eternal life."

Thankfully, we don't always get what we deserve.

Undeserved Forgiveness

I like to think I'm a pretty good driver. To this day, I've never received a speeding ticket. (Maybe that's because they've never been able to catch me, but that's another story.)

However, I *did* get pulled over once by a police officer for driving with an expired car tag. I tried to make my eyes look as huge and puppylike as I could. But his pen came out anyway, and he wrote me a ticket.

A few weeks later, I went to traffic court. I don't know if you've ever been to traffic court, but it's humiliating. The judge walked in and glared down at the teeming mass of lawbreakers. He walked up to his bench and assumed his thronelike position, high above the commoners. When he called a name, a person would rise from their place and approach his bench. Person after person offered their elaborate explanations and excuses, each coming to the same inevitable conclusion: "I wasn't at fault, Your Honor, and therefore I should not be required to pay this fine."

And the judge announced, person after person, that they must pay what they owe.

Finally, my turn came. "Mr. GROW-shell, please come forward."

As I walked across the room, I could hear people whispering around me, "Isn't that the pastor of Life Church?"

Busted.

The judge looked at me for a moment, then asked loudly, "So ... what's *your* story?"

I looked down at my feet, ashamed. I muttered quietly, barely above a whisper, "I was driving without a current tag."

The judge sat up straight in his throne. He looked at me sternly and asked, more enthusiastically, "What did you just say?!"

It's not bad enough I have to pay for my ticket. Now he's going to humiliate me, I thought. I glanced up to meet his eyes and realized that he had a pleasant expression, his eyebrows raised, his mouth slightly open. The look on his face seemed to be saying, *Work with me on this.*

I locked my eyes with his, straightened my back, and boldly raised my head. "Yes, Your Honor. You heard me correctly. I ... am ... guilty."

"Tell me your story," he said simply.

I explained, clearly, succinctly. "I'm very sorry, Your Honor, but I'm an idiot. I don't have any excuses. I simply forgot to renew my tag."

He had exactly what he needed. "Excuse me. Did you say you're an idiot?"

I responded in the affirmative.

"Are you a *guilty* idiot?" he asked, shooting me a look that clearly said, *Keep playing along.* I couldn't help smiling. It was funny.

He nodded exaggeratedly as he said, "I'll bet you're *very* sorry for what you did wrong."

I mirrored his exaggerated nod. "Yes, sir. What I did was wrong. Very wrong. And I am sorry. Very sorry. I am guilty."

Again, he had what he needed. The judge announced mockingly, loud enough for everyone to hear, "We've got this guilty person standing in a room full of innocent people. I've got to quickly get this guilty idiot out of here before he corrupts the rest of you innocent people. Craig Groeschel, you are free to go. You don't have to pay your fine. It's all forgiven."

Woo hoo! I danced all the way out to my car.

Let's review. Was I guilty? Of course I was. Did I deserve punishment? Again, yes. But did I have to pay for my crime? No! Why? Because the judge gave me grace. I didn't get what I deserved. I was forgiven. And this is exactly what God does for us. If we are "in Christ," he doesn't treat us as our sins deserve. God says in Isaiah 43:25, "I, even I, am he who blots out your transgressions, for my own sake, and remembers your sins no more."

Bad things do happen to good people. But Jesus' story is the ultimate good news story. Bad things happened to him so that good things could happen to us. I'm usually quick to ask why something bad happens. Rarely do I stop to ask why God might bless me with something good. The truth is, good things happen to people like you and me, people who are sinful and deserve death.

If you're hurting deeply right now, keep Job's story in mind. Even though he suffered immensely, in the end, God blessed him more than he had ever imagined. I pray that God will do the same for you. No matter what, we can be thankful to God that he doesn't always give us what we deserve. When it comes to our sins, thank God that he is *not* fair.

You Don't Have to Understand

When we don't understand something about God, some people are tempted to discredit him completely. My friend Andy Stanley said, "You don't have to understand everything to believe in something." In John 9, Jesus met a man who was born blind and forced to beg just to get by. Jesus' disciples wanted to know whose fault it was that the man was blind: Was it his fault? Or his parents?

For some reason, it's human nature to place blame. For example, if someone gets cancer, some Christian Atheists might wonder, *What do you think they did to deserve cancer?* If someone's wife walks out, insensitive churchgoers might think, *If he had been a better spiritual leader, his wife wouldn't have done that.* If a teenager is rebellious, hardened onlookers might privately reflect, *If that kid's parents had been more involved, this never would have happened.* People like to place blame.

When the disciples wondered who to blame, to their surprise Jesus answered, "Neither this man nor his parents sinned ... but this happened so that the work of God might be displayed in his life" (John 9:3). This man had spent years enduring the hardships of a life without sight, and Jesus basically said that God would be glorified through this tragedy. God can have a purpose in our pain.

Just because God can use what happens doesn't mean he causes everything. God does cause some pain (Heb. 12:7 – 11 talks about God "disciplining" his children), but much pain — especially that caused by the sins of other people — is not caused by God. He may *allow* it, but he doesn't *cause* it. That's an important distinction. Recognizing this fact might still leave us angry with him (and I'm guessing he probably understands when it's a person in pain). We learn to overcome this anger as we get to know God. And as we do, we learn how to trust that he is still good, loving, and wise in everything he does, even if we don't know why things happen.

Purpose in Our Pain

Even though many things in life will always hurt and be unexplainable, God occasionally (perhaps often) shines purposeful light into our darkness. If you're hurting right now, that might be difficult to believe. You might be in a place similar to where Michael and Andrea were when they lost their newborn child. Andrea begged me not to tell her that her baby died for a reason. In the moment, her objection to being given a reason was understandable, completely justified. But after a season of grieving, many find comfort in knowing that God can use even tragedies to bring about good. In fact, Ephesians 1:11 makes a bold statement: "[God] works out everything in conformity with the purpose of his will."

This is precisely what God did in the story of the man who was born blind. When Jesus saw him, he spit on the ground, made some mud with the saliva, and put it on the man's eyes. That doesn't make sense to our limited minds, and the man's lifetime of blindness up to that point certainly wasn't fair. But after washing in the Pool of Siloam, that man went home seeing.

This is the place where the story should reach its climactic ending. "Woo hoo! The blind guy can see now. Let's throw him a party. We'll eat cake and ice cream." And there was great rejoicing.

But that's not what happened. Jesus had performed an incredible miracle, but the Pharisees (religious leaders) wouldn't buy it because Jesus had done it on the Sabbath. Pharisees know: you can't work on the Sabbath. And *everybody* knows: healing is work. Because they didn't understand, they refused to believe.

After a great commotion, the Pharisees subpoenaed the

previously blind guy to ask him some more questions. With blunt honesty and clear sight, he said, "Whether [Jesus] is a sinner or not, I don't know. One thing I do know. I was blind but now I see!" (John 9:24 – 25). In other words, "Look guys, there are many things I don't claim to understand. But one thing is undeniably true: I was blind and now I see!" As a struggling Christian Atheist, I have my doubts and questions about God, but I'm thankful that just like the blind guy who was healed, I don't have to understand everything to believe something. If you're grieving, I pray that one day in the future, God will show you some purpose and meaning for your pain.

Life out of Death

On Christmas Eve in 2004, David Fox was admitted to the hospital. David was thirty-four and married, the father of one son. Even as David's health declined, hundreds of faithful Christians prayed for him, believing God for his full recovery. Certainly God would heal this passionate worship leader, godly father, faithful husband, and friend. We were all convinced David would come home.

On January 14, 2005, David died.

David wasn't just some guy at my church. He was my wife's only brother. Losing him was very personal to our family.

To say that we questioned God would be a massive understatement. Why would God allow this? Why would God take someone so young? Why didn't God answer our prayers?

What did any of us do to deserve this? Where is God in our pain and loss?

We grieved deeply, as you'd expect. The time at the funeral home was kind of a blur. I remember unlimited hugs from loved ones and unstoppable tears. I'll never forget when David's dad and my father-in-law, Sam, said to me, "Your children are never supposed to go before you." Losing his son brought this strong man to his knees. I prayed that I would never know the pain of losing a child.

At David's funeral, in the midst of our significant loss, we all tried to celebrate the good things from David's life. At the end of the service, I invited people in the crowd to meet the same Jesus who had changed David several years before. We have an uncle we call Uncle Blue. For years we had been praying that Uncle Blue would meet Christ. The more we asked God to reveal himself to our uncle, the farther he seemed to move away from God. When Uncle Blue accepted Christ at David's funeral, we were all speechless. To this day, Uncle Blue is a different person. His story is just one of many lives impacted by God for good — through David's death.

Even though we grieved deeply and didn't understand, God did something beautiful in our pain. God took our worst nightmare and somehow brought spiritual life out of a tragic death.

Even in the middle of our pain, or, perhaps more accurate, *especially* in the middle of our pain, God is good. If you are hurting and can't see his goodness now, I pray you will one day soon.

CHAPTER 6

When You Believe in God but Won't Forgive

When my little sister, Lisa, was born on my third birthday, my parents told me that she was my birthday present from God. We've been inseparable ever since. Of course we endured occasional sibling rivalries and conflicts, but she was always my baby sis, whom I loved as much as anyone else in the world. She still is.

I always believed I was her protector. Like a mother lion protecting her cubs, I was the big brother looking out for his little sis. Truthfully, there were times I enjoyed my protective role a bit too much — like the time I conveniently sat on the front porch cleaning my shotgun when her boyfriend came to pick her up. For some reason, that guy didn't stick around very long.

You can imagine how I felt when I learned of the tragedy. I found out that my little sister had been molested for years by a close family friend. Max had been Lisa's sixth-grade teacher. He taught me to play racquetball, shopped at my dad's retail store, and often cheered for my sister at her school drill-team performances. At the time, this single man in his midthirties seemed like a nice person looking for friends. Our family readily accepted him, unaware that behind the supportive teacher facade was a very sick man who repeatedly abused numerous girls over many years.

To say that I wanted Max to die and burn in hell doesn't even begin to convey how much I wanted him to suffer. Although the words *rage, hate,* and *revenge* come to mind when I think about Max, the English language simply doesn't have a word for what I felt.

We all know Christians are supposed to forgive. But many of us Christian Atheists think that there are exceptions to this rule. Sure, we should forgive most of the time — maybe even *almost all* of the time. But forgive a guy like Max?

Forget about it.

Bitterness

Hopefully you've never experienced something that hurt you as deeply as Max hurt our family. Unfortunately, chances are good that you have or that someone you know has. By some accounts, one in three girls and one in four boys in America will be victims of sexual abuse. (The odds are grossly higher in certain other parts of the world.) And sexual abuse is one of countless different kinds of betrayal. You might have confided in someone who betrayed your trust. Perhaps a close friend gossiped about you or cheated you out of money. Maybe your spouse lived a secret life and crushed you. If you're like many, one or both of your parents did something that deeply disappointed you. Perhaps right now you're reeling in pain from being trampled by someone you loved and trusted.

After the raw shock of discovering Max's abuse of my sister, one feeling festered inside me: bitterness. Truthfully, feeling bitter felt right. What else should I feel? After what he did to so many innocent little girls, he should suffer like they suffered, right? One day Max will get what's coming to him.

As a Christian Atheist, I felt justified in my bitter hatred, but the Bible clearly illustrates the danger of this natural response. One verse in Hebrews is easy to miss. It's tucked between one verse about holiness and another about sexual purity. Hebrews 12:15 says, "See to it that no one misses the grace of God and that no bitter root grows up to cause trouble and defile many."

The root of bitterness grows in the soil of hurt that has not been dealt with properly. Unknown to me, a root of bitterness started to grow in my heart. Roots absorb and store, and my heart absorbed and stored hurt, anger, hatred, and thoughts of revenge. Love keeps no record of wrongs, but bitterness keeps detailed accounts. And that's what I did. Over and over I played the story in my mind. Each time I pictured Max, my hatred grew.

Soon the root of bitterness started to push shoots out into my life. The verse in Hebrews warns that this bitter root can "cause trouble and defile many." My sister was permanently scarred by this cruel offense. As her brother, I took her offense as my own and allowed her wound to stain, pollute, and contaminate my heart. Bitterness is frighteningly easy to justify. *Since I've been wronged, I have a right to feel this way.*

When the target of our bitterness suffers, we celebrate their misfortunes. After all, they are getting what they deserve. When we found out that Max had been diagnosed with muscular dystrophy, I naturally concluded God was giving him his due. But when anyone celebrates another person's being diagnosed with a crippling disease, it's time for a heart check.

The longer I allowed the root of bitterness to live, the harder it was to kill. The root bored deeper, and the poison spread.

Killing the Root

When you pull a weed from the ground, if you don't get the roots, the weed will return. So it is with bitterness. Fortunately, Scripture shows us how to kill the root of bitterness. And unfortunately, we Christian Atheists are often skilled at avoiding this spiritual medicine. According to Ephesians 4:31 – 32, the only way to eliminate the root of bitterness is forgiveness. "Get rid of all bitterness, rage and anger, brawling and slander, along with every form of malice. Be kind and compassionate to one another, forgiving each other, just as in Christ God forgave you."

Forgiving is easier said than done, of course. Only God's power can bring us to a place of being willing to forgive. How could human willpower even begin to *want* to forgive someone like Max?

A medieval story captures the manner in which bitterness held me prisoner. Long ago, two monks were traveling and approached an unusually rough river. Standing alone on the bank was a woman who approached the monks and asked if they could help her cross so she could return home to her family. Knowing it was forbidden to touch a woman, one monk quickly looked the other way, ignoring her request for help.

The other monk, feeling compassion for the desperate lady, decided to bend the rules. Breaking tradition, he lifted her into his arms and carried her safely across the rushing water. Exceedingly grateful, the lady thanked the helpful monk and left for home.

The two monks continued on their journey. After miles of silence, the first monk finally said with disgust, "I can't believe you picked up that woman! You know we're never supposed to touch the opposite sex."

The compassionate monk replied, "I put her down miles ago, yet you continue to carry her in your heart."

That's exactly what I did with Max's betrayal. Month after month, year after year, I continued to carry the wound, refusing to put it down.

Praying for the Miracle

As I sat in church one Sunday, my pastor preached a convicting message on forgiveness, explaining how we should release those who've wronged us. As he read the words from Scripture commanding me to forgive, everything in me screamed, *No! I don't want to forgive Max! I refuse to release him!*

My pastor preached on. And God ever-so-slowly chipped away at the rough edges of my heart. As church neared its end, I walked alone to the altar to ask God for his help to forgive. I remember telling God that I knew I should forgive this man I hated, but I didn't want to. And even if I did want to, I wouldn't know how to forgive such a wrong.

The next week, in my personal Bible study, I came across a verse that helped to soften my heart a bit more. In Luke 6:28, Jesus teaches us to "bless those who curse you, pray for those who mistreat you." *I'm supposed to pray for those who mistreat me? Sure, I'll pray for Max. I'll ask God to give him a case of eternal hemorrhoids.* I certainly wasn't ready to pray for anything good.

Later I stumbled across another one of Jesus' annoying commands. This one is found in Matthew 5:43 – 44, where Jesus says, "You have heard that it was said, 'Love your neighbor and hate your enemy.' But I tell you: Love your enemies and pray for those who persecute you." There it was again — love and pray for your enemies!

Knowing I couldn't ignore this command any longer, I tried to pray for Max. In all honesty, I didn't pray that God would bless him in every way. I didn't ask that God would shower his love upon Max with a godly wife, healthy children, and a long and prosperous life. At the same time, I didn't ask God to torture him eternally in hell. In sheer obedience to God, I simply prayed a grudging but obedient three-second prayer: "God, I pray you work in his life."

Over the weeks and months, I continued uttering those same words. At first it was as painful as walking barefoot on burning coals. But eventually it became more bearable. Then I actually started to mean what I was praying. *God, work in his life.*

When we're told to pray for those who've hurt us, I'm convinced our prayers are as much for ourselves as they are for the offender. As God has helped me move beyond my Christian Atheist doubts about prayer, now I see an added value of praying for those who hurt me. My prayers for others may or may not change them. But my prayers always change me.

Praying for Max over time changed me. It made me a different person, so different that I began to contemplate the impossible: asking God to help me forgive Max.

Reluctant Forgiveness

I knew I was supposed to forgive Max for what he did to my sister, but I honestly didn't have a clue how to do it. God had convicted me and convinced me to begin — *God, I pray you work in his life* — but Max's actions still seemed unforgivable. How can a responsible grown man knowingly and repeatedly lure young girls into sexual abuse? How can he strip away their innocence? And how can I forgive that?

The answer is simple, but the farthest thing from easy. Colossians 3:13 teaches us to "forgive as the Lord forgave you."

God has forgiven us freely and completely, without any strings attached. And that's how we're supposed to forgive others. In what's now known as the Lord's Prayer, Jesus taught us to pray, "Forgive us our sins, for we also forgive everyone who sins against us" (Luke 11:4).

I was torn between wanting to obey God and wanting just as much to continue hating. I wrestled mightily in prayer with these verses. Still swimming in a pool of pain and bitterness, I decided it was time to try to forgive Max. Notice I used the word "decided." This was a decision based on my choice to obey Scripture, not a decision based on whether I felt like forgiving. Nothing in me felt like forgiving, but I still made the choice to try.

By faith, I asked God to help me forgive Max for what he'd done to my sister. By faith, I told God that I released Max from his sin. My prayer didn't feel sincere, but at least I was trying. Daily I bounced between wanting to forgive and wanting revenge. By nothing short of the power of God, I finally started to believe forgiveness was possible.

I can't overstate what God had to do in my heart to get me to this point. A grown man had maliciously abused my little sister — a sixth-grade girl. He cruelly groomed and preyed on other innocent children. This predator never apologized. He never attempted to right his wrongs. He never begged for our forgiveness.

My heart was stone hard. And only God could soften it to the point that I could even consider forgiving this molester. Miraculously, that's what God did. To this day, I don't know exactly how or when it happened. But it did. By God's grace, I had forgiven Max for his sin and abuse. With God's help I'd done the humanly impossible, and I felt as though a spiritual weight had been lifted. The Bible became clearer. God seemed nearer. My heart was purer.

One Christmas, when I was visiting my parents, I decided to write Max a letter expressing my forgiveness. The task wasn't easy, but that's often par for the course. In the letter, I explained how much God had forgiven me. I told Max the story of Jesus and his love for us. I explained that I had forgiven him and that God could as well. I included a short prayer he might pray, asking Jesus to heal his heart and forgive his sins.

I didn't realize that Max's sickness had advanced. He was losing the battle with muscular dystrophy. In fact, at the time he received the letter, Max was under the care of a hospice nurse, waiting for inevitable death.

Months after Max passed away, his nurse sent us a letter asking if she could talk to us. When we agreed, she told us about the last days of Max's life, believing we needed to know. The caregiver explained that Max's eyesight had deteriorated and that he had asked her to read him my note. Although she wasn't aware of what he had done (and I never told her), it was obvious to her that he had done something grievously wrong. According to the nurse, he listened with tears streaming down his face. He asked her to pray the prayer with him. She recalled that his whole countenance changed as he asked Christ to forgive him and make him new. He died a few days later.

We Christian Atheists can rationalize as many excuses as

we need to avoid forgiving. We *Christians*, however, can find in God the sheer strength to battle through the feelings of anger, hatred, and bitterness, and fight our way back to the cross. That's where Christ forgave us. And that's where, by faith, we can find the ability to forgive those who've wronged us.

CHAPTER 7

When You Believe in God but Don't Think You Can Change

"THIS IS JUST THE WAY I AM," I CONFIDENTLY TOLD MY counselor. "I can't change."

At the tender age of twenty-six, I was a candidate to become fully ordained. Several leaders who were overseeing my journey toward ordination were convinced that I was a workaholic and needed help to change. I was convinced they were wrong. *They just don't know how much I care about God and his church*, I rationalized. This wise and caring panel of ministers asked me to take a week off to contemplate my priorities and consider what changes I could make that would give me the endurance to go the distance. Knowing this was a battle I wouldn't win, I agreed to take some time off, although I honestly never planned to follow through and slow my frenzied pace.

When they inevitably discovered that I didn't take the week off but instead continued working feverishly, they assigned me to mandatory counseling to address my workaholic tendencies. I found myself sitting quietly in a little chair, facing a well-intentioned counselor. He reviewed his notes, mumbled a little to himself, looked up at me, and said, "You really don't think you can change, huh?" Just like I didn't think I could ever forgive Max, I also didn't believe I could change my work habits. Convinced that this was just the way I was, I explained (again) how I couldn't lessen my drive to work. I'll never forget what happened next. He leaned in, and lovingly, not much above a whisper, said, "So ... what you're telling me is, even our God isn't big enough to help you change?"

He got me.

Identifying the Lie

Many Christian Atheists live year after year under the illusion that we simply can't change. Once we've forgiven ourselves for past mistakes, some surrender to present problems, never even hoping to overcome them. We may openly, even proudly, believe in God, but we honestly don't believe he can change us. And it's not that we've never tried to change. We have — often. Perhaps we prayed and asked God for help, but nothing happened. Or we read a book, listened to a sermon, or accepted advice from a trusted friend, only to end up in the same place we started. Maybe we made a New Year's resolution, joined a support group, even visited a counselor, all hoping to change. But when we didn't succeed, we eventually surrendered our hopes for a different life. *Even though I believe in God, I don't*

really think he can help. After all, this is how he made me.
Maybe, like the apostle Paul, this is simply the thorn in my flesh.

Many believe a common lie. A lie believed as truth will affect you as if it were true. I have this friend — let's call him Jeremy — who's addicted (in no particular order) to alcohol, porn, sleeping with girls, and smoking pot. Although Jeremy has been a Christian since he was fifteen years old, his life certainly isn't moving forward. Each week, Jeremy faithfully sits on the fourth row at church, convinced that he can never overcome his addictions. In his mind, this makes him unworthy of God's love.

Jeremy doesn't believe he'll ever change. I know God can change Jeremy, but it won't happen as long as he believes it won't. Jeremy lives inside an invisible fence. I have another friend, Robert, whose dog, Sadie, kept running away. Robert installed a wire underground that would trigger a small shock in Sadie's collar each time she'd approach the yard's edge. It took several escape attempts to train her, but now Sadie lives within her invisible rectangle. It's like a little doggie Bermuda Triangle in the yard: Sadie can never escape it. That was years ago, and Sadie no longer wears her shock collar. But she's so well-conditioned that, to this day, she avoids the edge of her property. In that dog's mind, there's still a barrier — even though none exists. Jeremy, like other Christian Atheists who've tried to change and failed, wrongly believes that God simply can't change him.

The apostle Paul had some strong words for the Corinthian church, which was struggling with all sorts of sinful behavior.

He explained that we battle with different weapons than the world uses: "For though we live in the world, we do not wage war as the world does. The weapons we fight with are not the weapons of the world. On the contrary, they have divine power to demolish strongholds" (2 Cor. 10:3 – 4). The Greek word translated as strongholds is *ochuroma* (pronounced oak-EW-ROH-muh), which means to fortify, lock up, or imprison. This is what our enemy tries to do to us. He lies to us until we're convinced that we're stuck and can never escape our problems. That's what happened to me and my workaholism. I believed that this was just the way I was made. *I'm driven to work hard. People who don't work hard are lazy and don't care as much as I do. I'll never change this about me.* My thoughts made me a prisoner. Like many other Christian Atheists, I believed the lie that I couldn't change.

Admitting to the Problem

In Romans 6:14, Paul said, "Sin shall not be your master." Yet many of us are mastered by things that aren't God's best for us. Many Christian friends close to me are mastered by something as innocent as caffeine. They can't make it to 9:00 a.m. without a serious shot (or double shot) of their favorite start-me-up drink. Several buddies of mine are hooked on dipping snuff. As much as they'd like to quit, they just can't. (They even admit that they know spitting in a cup is not sexy.) Many great people are addicted to smoking cigarettes or cigars. People around the world depend on alcohol or drugs just to cope with daily life.

Some can't stop gambling. Others can't stop spending. Many can't stop lusting. Still others can't stop eating. Even technology holds some people hostage. I know otherwise normal people who can't go thirty minutes without checking email, Facebook, or Twitter. They have been mastered and don't even know it. Worse, they believe it's impossible for them to change.

Some are simply bound by a false belief. They think they aren't good with people and never will be. Or they're convinced that they'll always have a negative attitude. Some believe they could never get in good physical shape. Others are convinced they're destined to remain in a meaningless job. They're imprisoned by false thoughts, all along believing they can never escape, never change. And then there are those who have serious problems but don't even know it. They too remain locked in a prison they're not even aware exists.

Whatever the challenge, the first step is often the most difficult. In my first round of counseling for my problem of overworking, I made little progress. "Craig, do you think you have a problem with working too much?" My counselor was digging for an honest answer from me.

I was convinced that I was simply dedicated to ministry. "No," I answered confidently, honestly. "I really don't believe I have a problem at all."

And I stood by that answer. Until Amy and I had our first child, Catie.

On Tuesday, March 15, 1996, I was teaching at a downtown lunch Bible study when my pager vibrated. I looked down to see my home number, followed by "911." This was the "your pregnant wife is probably going into labor, so you'd better call immediately" signal that Amy and I had worked out in advance. I dropped everything and hammered my '89 Honda Accord like it was Speed Racer's Mach 5. Turns out, we had time. After eight hours of labor, we proudly held our first daughter, Catie Elizabeth. It was Wednesday, March 16, 1996, and life was perfect — or so I thought.

Amy was recovering quickly, and little Catie was really healthy, so the doctors said we could go home on Friday. Unfortunately, I was enrolled in a seminary class that met all day Friday and Saturday. Now, this wasn't just any ordinary class. It was *the* class, the one that was going to save me an extra semester and help me graduate by the end of the year. Not wanting to miss class and jeopardize my impending graduation, I decided someone else could drive Amy and our beautiful firstborn infant home from the hospital. (In case you're wondering, this was Stupid Mistake 1.)

As I attended class all day that Friday, I smugly marveled at my own dedication, my wholehearted commitment that would eventually lead our family to an early graduation, secure in the knowledge that I had made impeccable arrangements to have my wife and my first daughter chauffeured home. That evening, I faithfully preached at our weekly Friday evening service. (An event now referenced as Stupid Mistake 2.) Saturday morning, I left before the sun rose to commute ninety minutes back to seminary, where I stayed the entire day. (Yes, this was number 3.) On Sunday morning, I preached three times and returned home to my wife and firstborn. You'll remember them from earlier in our story — the two women I cared most for in the world, whom I'd left to fend for themselves during the first sixty hours at home together. (Sunday's decision accounted for mistakes 4, 5, and 6 — and that was just in three days!) Obviously, I'm still alive today, but that's only by the grace of God and through Amy's mercy. Some people don't believe it, but before Catie's birth, Amy and I had honestly never had an argument. On that Sunday afternoon, I walked in the door sincerely believing I'd been an ideal husband. After three flawless years of marriage, we made up for lost time and had a fight that is still echoing somewhere over a small house on NW 16th Street.

Okay, so maybe I did have a small problem with being a workaholic. I was finally ready to acknowledge that I — possibly — needed help. Over time, I began to realize that my problem wasn't so small. For some reason, I was consumed with a need to work. I was the first person to the office, the last to leave. I ignored days off like a head cheerleader ignores catcalls from freshmen. Vacations were for wimps. Time away from work was for people who weren't dedicated. I had to work the hardest. And it wasn't just the work; I had to produce, to be the best.

Looking back, I can now acknowledge that I was trying to prove something, to compensate for my own feelings of unworthiness. This unhealthy need overtook every other part of my life. Addictions are idolatry. We're trying to meet some need that only Christ can, looking to anything but him. I was trying to prove my worth in production, rather than finding value in Christ alone. Admitting that took more work (and pain) than I can describe. Too many Christian Atheists won't acknowledge their problem in the first place. I wouldn't for years. We can always find plenty of excuses why it isn't that big of a deal. But if we won't admit our problems, we can't change.

God Can Help You Change

Admitting our problems is only the first step. After that, we must invite God to work, because he is the one who can change any problem. When Jesus was explaining how difficult it is for a rich man to enter heaven, his disciples were taken aback. They wondered who could possibly be saved. Jesus replied, "With man this is impossible, but not with God; all things are possible with God" (Mark 10:27). With people, change may be difficult, even impossible — but not with God. God is bigger than our problems, no matter what they are. If you've believed that you simply can't change, acknowledge that that is a lie. With God, all things are possible.

For example, my wife always believed she was a night person. Unquestionably, Amy came to life at the end of the day. Mornings were another story. Her family warned me before we married, "Don't talk to her until she's been awake for awhile, or you're taking your life into your own hands." They were exaggerating — a little.

After we were married, holding jobs, and starting a family, rising early became more important for Amy to be successful in her roles. Her whole life, she'd been told she wasn't a morning person. During her prayer time, she realized God could change her. She told me she was praying that God would make her better in the morning. Almost overnight, Amy changed. Like sunlight bursting suddenly through dark clouds, Amy's mornings transformed. Even when others didn't believe change was possible, Amy did. More important, God did.

Many Christian Atheists give up hope. *I tried to change, but I can't. Nothing ever works for me. You don't understand. This is just the way I am.* It's time to reject the lies of the evil one and embrace the truth of God. If you'll allow God to change you, I'll share a few steps my counselor showed me to allow God to be bigger than any earthly master.

Ask Yourself

When working with people who think they can't change, I ask six simple questions. If a person answers yes to three or more, chances are they have a problem.

1. *Do your family and friends say you have a problem?*
   Even though you might deny it, others can often see more objectively than you.

2. *Do you continue even though you are hurting people?*
   If you look at what some people claim has control over you, do you keep practicing or giving in to it, even when it affects others negatively? You don't want to hurt people. But if they continue to suffer because of your actions, chances are good that you have a problem.

3. *Do you arrange your schedule, priorities, or spending around it?* If you make major life changes to get your "fix," odds are, your fix has a strong hold on you.

4. *Can you go one week without it?* When I couldn't go one week without work, it became obvious I had a problem. If you can't walk away from something for a week, you're in bondage to that thing.

5. *Is it driving others away?* Once an addiction reaches advanced stages, it tends to isolate the one who's addicted. When your actions continually hurt, abuse, or neglect others, they tend to pull back.

6. *Are you denying it is a problem or trying to keep it a secret?* If you feel defensive, adamantly insisting that you don't have a problem, you likely have a problem. If you're hiding some behavior from others, there's a reason. You need to address it head-on instead.

At the height of my workaholism, I answered yes to five of these six questions. Unfortunately, even after Catie's birth jerked me into realizing I had a problem, I wasn't ready to change — yet.

Can the Excuses

Before you begin your journey toward change, brace yourself. The excuse monster is waiting in the shadows, ready to rear his ugly head: *I've tried before. Nothing works for me. I've done everything possible and can't change. This is just the way I am. It's not that big of a deal. Lots of people have bigger problems than I do.*

Before you can tap into God's life-changing power, you have to eliminate the excuses. Jesus approached a pool surrounded by many sick people, where he discovered a man who'd been an invalid for thirty-eight years. The Bible says, "When Jesus saw him lying there and learned that he had been in this condition for a long time, he asked him, 'Do you want to get well?'" (John 5:6). That question seems so simple. "Do you want to get well?" That's like asking a broke man, "Hey, you want a million dollars?" Instead of getting excited — "Yes, I want to be well!" — this man responded with an excuse. "'Sir,' the invalid replied, 'I have no one to help me into the pool when the water is stirred. While I am trying to get in, someone else goes down ahead of me'" (v. 7).

This hurting man was offered the opportunity to see God's power. But he had grown so accustomed to his condition that he was focused on all the reasons he'd never get better. So many people are like that. I was too. As our family and ministry grew, so did my work addiction. People who loved me often expressed concern about my work schedule. Since I'd already been to counseling, I was convinced it didn't work. I knew all the reasons why I'd never change.

Another experience with my firstborn daughter finally deflated all my excuses — once and for all. Catie was almost two, and I had been on an unusually long stretch of work. According to Amy, it was my fifteenth consecutive night away from home on some (incredibly important) church assignment. I dashed in the house to change clothes, already running behind for a business meeting. On my way out, I scooped up Catie to kiss her goodbye and said enthusiastically, "I hope to be home in time to kiss you goodnight." Beautiful Catie's piercing blue eyes blinked back at me. "But Daddy, you don't live at our house. You live at the church." Her honesty knocked the breath out of me. I had to acknowledge my problem and overcome all my lame excuses. It was way past time.

If you have any excuses talking you out of changing, capture those wrong thoughts and replace them with truth. Paul said, "We demolish arguments and every pretension that sets itself up against the knowledge of God, and we take captive every thought to make it obedient to Christ" (2 Cor. 10:5). Grab any thought contrary to God's, overtake it, and replace it with truth.

When you are tempted to think, *Both of my parents are heavy, so I'll always struggle with my weight,* stop. Remind yourself that you can do all things through Christ who gives you strength (Phil. 4:13). With God's help, you can lose weight. You think, *I'm just not good with money. I'll always be in debt.* Capture that and instead say, *God is teaching me to be faithful with all I have. I am not what I have. I am who God says I am. One day I'll be totally debt-free* (Luke 16:10; Rom. 13:8). You catch yourself thinking, *Some people are positive people. I'm not. I'm just naturally critical and negative.* That's not true. Instead remind yourself that you have the mind of Christ. God is renewing your mind daily (1 Cor. 2:16; Rom. 12:2). When you feel bad about yourself and start sliding into those all-too-familiar thoughts, remember that if you follow Christ, the same spirit that raised Christ from the dead lives inside of you (Rom. 8:9 – 11). You are created in God's image (Gen. 1:27). He knew you before you were born (Ps. 139:13 – 16). He has grand designs for you, great works that he planned in advance for you to do (Eph. 2:10).

If you're not dead, you're not done. God still has something important for you to do. These truths alone make you important. You can change. Capture wrong thoughts and replace them with truth. Can the excuses. If you keep making excuses, you're insulting God's power. With God, all things are possible — even the thing that you think isn't.

Immediately after the man who'd been paralyzed for thirty-eight years offered his excuse, Jesus revealed his power. "Then Jesus said to him, 'Get up! Pick up your mat and walk.' At once the man was cured; he picked up his mat and walked" (John 5:8 – 9).

Cut the Ties

As you overcome any excuses that may hold you back, you'll also want to cut any ties that might hold you down. The apostle Paul said, "Do not be misled: 'Bad company corrupts good character'" (1 Cor. 15:33). If you're surrounded by naysayers or others dangerous to your progress, ditch them. Surround yourself with new friends, good friends.

For example, if you're overcoming your problem with lust, and your buddies are going to strip clubs or have pornographic magazines lying around in their apartments, you need new friends. If you're determined to drop thirty pounds, but your friend Alicia keeps showing up with two pints of Ben and Jerry's Triple Caramel Chunk ice cream, Alicia needs to go. If you're striving to please God with your life, but the person you're dating continues to push you to do things you know you shouldn't, it's time to throw that little fish back into the pond.

Amy and I once realized that we were becoming prideful about our ministry, and increasingly critical about others. Every time we'd hang out with certain close friends, we'd find ourselves talking about how ineffective other ministries were. Our prideful attitude was growing. *Our way is best. Everyone else is doing it wrong.* We knew our attitudes were displeasing to God, but we continued becoming negative and critical of others. We tried to explain to our friends that we didn't want to criticize others, but they didn't get it. When we realized that we were allowing our friends to influence us negatively, we decided to gently distance ourselves. We started hanging around different friends. It may sound cruel, but "bad company corrupts good morals." If you honestly want to change, surround yourself with people who will help, people who believe you can do it.

Surrender to God's Power

If you believe you can't change, you're right — sort of. Your strength is limited. Your willpower isn't bottomless. Your determination will eventually run dry. That's why to change for good you need the power of the only one who is good — Christ!

In Colossians 1:29, Paul says, "To this end I labor, struggling with all his energy, which so powerfully works in me." The word translated as "struggling" is the Greek word *agonizomai* (ag-oh-NID-zohm-ah-hee). It means to struggle or compete for a prize. It literally means to compete with an adversary — and win. It's important to notice how we're supposed to struggle, to fight. The Bible says we *agonizomai* with "*all* Christ's energy." We change by *his* power, not by ours.

One time I was at the gym with my longtime friend and workout partner John. We were exercising our chest muscles, and at the end of our workout, we each decided to do a "burn out" set of bench presses. To exhaust our already fatigued muscles, we put a very low weight on a long bar and lay down on a bench. I went first. I pushed the bar easily off my chest before letting it drop slowly down. Because it was such low weight, I was able to lift a quick twenty reps. What started easy quickly became more difficult. As I strained to continue, John gently grabbed the bar to support me. He cheered me on each time I managed to thrust the bar successfully off my chest. "Come on, Groesch! It's all you!" he shouted, encouraging me to continue. When the weight became too much for my exhausted pectorals, John grabbed the bar with both his hands.

Standing over my body, he held a portion of the weight, still allowing me to work. Lifting about half the weight for me, John continued to shout, "Keep going! Don't stop! It's all you!" Each time I pushed up, a little more strength left my body, and John carried a little more weight for me. As he continued to cheer me on, he kept saying, "It's all you! It's all you, man!" Exhausted, I finally let go of the bar. John didn't notice. He continued lifting the bar for about five more reps, still shouting, "It's all you! It's all you!"

When he looked down and saw me smiling up at him, we both started laughing.

"Good set, Groesch. Good burn. You're the man."

Change won't just take all the strength you have; it will take more. You need God's power. Do what you can, and trust God to do what you can't.

In my second round of counseling, I finally admitted I was a workaholic. No longer reluctantly, I acknowledged that my problem could endanger my health and the well-being of my family. My wise Christian counselor helped me see that I'm addicted to adrenaline.

Instead of finding my worth in what I produce, I'm finding my worth in who I am in Christ. Although I certainly haven't arrived, everyone around me will tell you that God has changed me. I am different because of his power. My day off is sacred. My time away is consistent. My devotional life is rich. And my family knows me. Instead of working fifteen nights straight, I'm at home six nights most weeks. Instead of traveling nonstop, preaching, I gladly limit my ministry trips to a dozen a year. Like my pastor friend said, "I won't sacrifice my family on the altar of ministry." I care for my family and for my body. And God has done more through the church when I've done less.

Learning how to rest and put my family first is hard. I still struggle often, and nothing in me is strong. Any success I've had is not because of my strength but because of God's power through my weakness. When Paul begged God to remove something from his life, God said, "My grace is sufficient for you, for my power is made perfect in weakness." Therefore, Paul says, "I will boast all the more gladly about my weaknesses, so that Christ's power may rest on me. That is why, for Christ's sake, I delight in weaknesses, in insults, in hardships, in persecutions, in difficulties. For when I am weak, then I am strong" (2 Cor. 12:9 – 10).

Can you overcome workaholism after one attempt? I certainly couldn't. But you can make an appointment with a counselor, read a good book, or close your laptop and go home on time today. If you find it hard to emotionally connect with your family, can you be the perfect parent or spouse by bedtime? Obviously not. But you can spend a few extra minutes listening to your six-year-old talk about bugs, hug your spouse, or write an encouraging note and leave it by your kids' toothbrushes. You may not be able to fix everything, but you can do *something*. Do what you can today. And rely on God to do what you can't.

You can't change in your own power. If you feel overwhelmed by something bigger than you, let the one who is bigger than all things be the power you need in your weakness.

CHAPTER 8

When You Believe in God but Still Worry All the Time

IT HAPPENED AGAIN THE OTHER NIGHT. I TRIED NOT TO LOOK at the clock, but every so often, I just couldn't resist: 1:12 a.m. I calculated precisely how much sleep I'd get if I could fall asleep now. What seemed just a few minutes later, I glanced again: 2:32 a.m. I adjusted my estimated sleep down an hour and twenty minutes. I wish I could tell you I was praying, meditating on Scripture, even simply basking in God's presence. But I wasn't. Though I was growing through my workaholic problems, I still had others. I was lying awake, sweating, drenched in worry.

It's amazing that one seemingly straightforward church decision could so profoundly haunt me. If I did what I felt was right, hundreds of people would be hurt; they'd simply never understand. But if I did nothing, my indecision would hurt even more people in the long run. Worry.

My mom had just been released from the hospital (for the second time) for a series of small strokes. She had lost much of her eyesight. At first, the doctors told her it would probably all come back. Then they changed their diagnosis, saying it wasn't likely to return at all. More worry.

Amy had battled chronic infections for years and was starting to get better. Then she suddenly got worse — much worse. Even more worry.

In the light of day, I'm constantly encouraging people to trust God, no matter what. I can quote Scripture from memory without taking a breath. But when the night sets in, I stare at the ceiling, feeling alone, afraid to trust God completely. If I can be truly honest, I am often overwhelmed with worry.

I know I'm not supposed to worry. I try not to worry, but sometimes it's hard. Worry is bad for our health. In fact, our word *worry* derives from the Old High German *wurgen*, literally "to strangle, constrict, choke." That sounds like worry feels, doesn't it? Worry absolutely strangles the life out of me. But there are just so many things to worry about, how can I stop? When there's nothing to worry about, I worry about that: *Uh-oh, things are too good right now. The other shoe's about to drop.* And since worry is bad for my health, I worry about that. How do I stop?

Christian Atheists can always find something to worry about. The economy is tight. Jobs are unstable. I know a lot of people right now who don't know how they're going to pay their bills. How are we going to do it all? The kids are growing up — college and weddings inevitably loom ahead. And as if the basics weren't enough — food, clothes, shoes, a roof over our heads — in the times we live in, how do we keep our kids safe? We can pray for them and try to protect them from outside influences. But we're going to have to let them go out there into the world eventually, and it's rough. Kids — little kids — are into porn and drugs and sex. We try to protect ours. But what about all the other kids they know? And even those from our church? Are their parents protecting them? Or are our kids' friends seeing things they shouldn't, then telling our kids about it?

Our kids aren't the only family members to worry about; we also have our aging parents who are starting to need us more. How are we going to care for them? What if they get sick?

Or maybe somebody we love, even someone who's always been healthy, has something unusual going on physically. So they visit the doctor for tests and are told the results will be back soon. That's when the waiting begins. Waiting gives us time to wonder, time to worry. I personally can't help but ask, *What if?* Then my mind races, keeping me awake at night. My chest hurts. My arms and legs twitch. I can't catch my breath, and it feels like worry is eating me from the inside out. I'm supposed to trust God, but it's often hard to do.

Then I worry about our church. Sometimes, I worry about my own abilities, even my motives: *Am I doing a good job? What if I mess up this message? What if some people spend eternity in hell because I didn't clearly present the gospel message? What if?*

Worry Is Not Your Friend

Worry (or not trusting God) has been a significant issue in my life. Although I believe in God, I've trusted more in my own abilities than I have in his faithfulness. For Christian Atheists, our worry proves we don't trust in God as we claim to. We think, *I know God's a good God and all that, but I've got this situation handled.* And when it turns out we don't have it handled, then it falls to us — not to God — to fix it.

Worry reminds me of my feelings about snakes. I hate snakes. I hate them worse than Indiana Jones does. It was a serpent that seduced all of mankind into the fall, after all. Coincidence? I think not. Snakes in general freak me out, but bringing venomous vipers into the equation adds another diabolical dimension. My family lives in a heavily wooded area, where we're basically besieged by poisonous snakes.

One day, when my son Bookie (whose real name is Stephen Craig) was about two years old, he was playing on our front porch. We were all doing different things around the yard when suddenly we heard Bookie squealing with delight. He was jumping up and down, calling out, "My fwend! My fwend! Daddy, look! He's my fwend!"

I strolled over and asked, "Bookie, where's your fwend? Is it an imaginary fwend?"

Bookie chirped, "No, Daddy!" and pointed excitedly. "Look! My fwend!" And there, directly at his feet, was a small rattlesnake. In case you didn't already know, a rattlesnake is not your fwend. I jerked Bookie away from the snake, then stomped on the snake's head and crushed it — immediately after I first cut off its head with a shovel.

Many of us treat worry like our fwend. We don't consciously think or talk about it that way, of course, but how we live tells a different story. We clutch worry to our chests like our favorite stuffed animals from childhood. We have many different euphemisms to mask this sin:

"I'm concerned about something."

"I have some issues I'm working through."

"I have a lot on my mind."

Using such substitute terminology makes me sound like I'm really smart, like I'm an important person with big things going on. What they don't do is make me sound like I'm a worrywart.

But no matter what you call it, worry is still sin. In Philippians 4:6, Paul tells us not to be anxious about anything. Romans 14:23 says, "Everything that does not come from faith is sin." That's pretty clear to me. Worry is the opposite of faith; therefore, it's sin.

When we live by faith, we believe that God has everything under control. But if we start to worry, how we live says the opposite. If we are worried about losing our jobs, we are essentially saying that our jobs are our providers. But isn't God our provider? What if God has something else planned for us? And what if, as unpleasant as it may be to think about, the path to that "something else" is through some pain? Will we still trust in God to provide during that time?

Worry, in essence, is the sin of distrusting the promises and the power of God. It's choosing to dwell on, to think about, the worst-case scenario. It's faith in the bad things rather than faith in God. Second Timothy 1:7 says, "God has not given us a spirit of fear and timidity, but of power, love, and self-discipline" (NLT). In this verse, you could also easily translate "fear and timidity" as "anxiety, tension, and worry." Fear doesn't come from God. It's a tool the evil one uses to distract us from our true purpose here.

In Matthew 6:25, Jesus says, "Do not worry about your life, what you will eat or drink; or about your body, what you will wear. Is not life more important than food, and the body more important than clothes?" The Greek word Jesus uses for "life" is *psuche* (SUE-kay). It doesn't just mean your breathing life, the force that makes your body go. It actually means every aspect of your life, taken together in total: mental, physical, emotional, and spiritual. It means your yesterday, today, and future life. Jesus is simply saying don't worry about anything.

The Christian Atheist may do everything humanly possible to ensure a situation's positive outcome, and still worry, *I can't just let this sit. I have to do more.* But if we've honestly done everything we can, by definition we can't do anything more. And in many cases nothing's going to go wrong anyway; there's really nothing you can do about a nonexistent worst-case scenario. So in our powerlessness we settle for the only thing left within our control: we worry.

Worry is a control issue. People are often obsessed with trying to control their circumstances. And while some things in life are within our ability, many things aren't.

Just last night I sat on a plane, hoping to make a connecting flight. As we were grounded on the runway, time seemed to fly, chipping away at my chances to make my connection. Even though I had zero control over the situation, I glanced continuously at my watch, consumed with worry — as if my worry had any bearing on the outcome. (In case you're wondering, after our plane landed, I could have given Usain Bolt a run for his money, sprinting across the airport just in time to catch my final leg home.)

Worry indicates we're not willing to let God handle certain things — at least not in his way, and certainly not in his time. Matthew 6:27 asks a practical question: "Who of you by worrying can add a single hour to his life?" I wonder how many hours worry has shaved off the end of my life? (Now I'm really worried.)

Fortunately, God's power and love have enabled me to genuinely overcome much of my worry and unjustified desire to control. I know I still have a long road ahead of me, but I'm going to share with you some of my journey so far.

Freedom from Worry

Two steps toward freedom from worry are to do what's wise and to think on the right things. As Christians, we can be tempted to "overdo faith." I put that in quotes because it would be more accurate to say it's "underdoing personal responsibility." There's really no way to have too much faith, assuming you understand faith the way God does. Some people think faith is doing nothing in order to let God do everything for them. For example, I have an out-of-work friend who believed that God was going to provide a new job for him.

I said, "So, have you been looking for a job?"

My friend said, "Nope."

"Well, do you have a resume?"

"Nope."

"Are you networking? Out trying to meet people?"

"Nope."

"Well, uh … what exactly are you doing?"

"I'm trying not to freak out while I'm hoping that God will bring me a job."

I've known many people like this in a variety of different situations. You probably have too.

"So you'd like to get married. Have you left the house? Talked to anyone of the opposite sex … ever?"

"Yes, no, and no. I'm waiting for God to bring her to my door."

Keep on waiting, Mr. Lucky.

Some people are always broke. "Do you have a plan?"

"Yeah, a friend of mine is going to get me some lotto tickets, and God's going to give me millions."

But God does give us responsibility, and it takes biblical faith to do those things in dependence on God. Scripture says over and over again, in as many ways as you can think to say it: do what's wise. Proverbs 9:12 says, "If you are wise, your wisdom will reward you."

Need a job? Put together a resume. Network. Make some phone calls. Iron a shirt for your next interview. That's wise.

Are you single and want to get married? Shower. Brush your teeth. Use mouthwash. Put on some nice clothes. Put on cologne. (Not too much!) Now leave your house. Get a nice haircut. Go someplace where moral, single people of the opposite sex hang out. Smile. Be nice. Be polite. Ask friends to introduce you to people. Don't stalk anyone. That's wise.

Are you always broke? Stop taking advice from your broke friends. Quit spending more than you make. Cut up your credit cards. Don't buy things you don't need with money you don't have. Start clawing your way out of debt.

Wisdom is all about the simple, often tiny, obvious things, done consistently, one at a time. Philippians 4:6 – 7 tells us, "Don't worry about anything." And it doesn't just tell us what *not* to do. It tells us what *to* do as well. "Don't worry about anything; instead, pray about everything. Tell God what you need, and thank him for all he has done. If you do this, you will experience God's peace, which is far more wonderful than the human mind can understand. His peace will guard your hearts and minds as you live in Christ Jesus" (NLT). That makes it sound so easy, but if we do what's wise, we can peacefully leave the rest to God.

If you do catch yourself worrying even after you've done what was wise, remember that God is bigger than our problems, and that he wants us to hand them over to him. Worry then becomes a signal alerting us that it's time to pray. Any time you hear the alarm start to blare, stop. It's time to stop worrying and start praying.

When we tell God what we're worried about or what

we need, we are giving our burden to him. We still have responsibility to do what we can, but doing what we can't isn't ours anymore. Anytime we try to take back God's responsibilities onto our shoulders, we remind ourselves, *Now that's his problem.* And we can breathe a sigh of relief. It's part of that supernatural peace he promised (Phil. 4:7).

Remember the "What if?" game I mentioned earlier? We've all experienced that. *What if my baby stops breathing in her sleep? What if I lose my job? What if I left my coffee pot turned on when I left the house this morning?* Okay, that last one might be a legitimate reason for a trip home or a quick phone call. But there's only so much you can do about the other two. When our minds begin to wander like that, we must learn to recognize and label worry for what it is. It is the alarm calling us to pray. We can start by telling ourselves, *This is not a God thought. This is a thought based on fear.* Then we must capture that runaway thought and make it obedient to Christ. Philippians 4:8 says, "Whatever is true, whatever is noble, whatever is right, whatever is pure, whatever is lovely, whatever is admirable — if anything is excellent or praiseworthy — think about such things." As we continue to pray, we can shift our minds from fear-based thinking to faith-based thinking.

Sometimes God's response to prayer may take longer than you want. Second Peter 3:8 – 9 says, "With the Lord a day is like a thousand years, and a thousand years are like a day. The Lord is not slow in keeping his promise, as some understand slowness." As we saw in the chapter on prayer, we pray with drive-through-window expectations. But God is far more patient than we are. He has eternity, so he's in no hurry. He's more like a "seven course sit-down dinner with friends for hours" kind of God. When we don't see immediate results to prayers, our tendency is to take back what we gave to God. But we can't. It was never ours in the first place. Worry is the result of trying to carry a burden that never belonged on our shoulders. If we Christian Atheists make this attempt, we're admitting we don't actually trust God. In our minds, our God is too small, and we must come to our own rescue.

Honestly, do you want your worry back? It's not your fwend. The promise of Philippians 4:7 is that when you give it to him, "you will experience God's peace, which is far more wonderful than the human mind can understand. His peace will guard your hearts and minds" (NLT). So stop worrying. And take advantage of what he's offering. Do what you can, and then trust God with what you cannot do: "Here you go, God. Say hello to my little fwend." Do what's wise and think on the right things.

Let's try a few simple dry runs. What if you or a loved one has cancer? What can you do? Well, you can go to a doctor, get advice, and pursue treatment. But ultimately, can you guarantee healing of the cancer? No. Can God? Yes. So give that one to God. If you do start to worry, that is your alarm to pray about it. In the end, you have to trust God to do what he's going to do.

Can you protect your kids from all danger? No. Can God give his angels charge over your kids? Yes. So do what you reasonably can to protect your kids, and give what you can't do to God.

Can you change your spouse? You hesitated; maybe you think you can. But you can't. Can God change your spouse? Yes. (And God can change you too, by the way. Just saying.) So give that one to God.

Can your worry change anything? No. Can God change anything? Absolutely he can. Do what God tells you to. Give everything you cannot do to God.

No Matter What Happens, Trust God

Some time ago, something really unusual happened. Our church had been around for twelve years, and then suddenly, for no apparent reason, financial contributions just tanked. The bottom fell out, essentially overnight. Now, revenue had dropped before, but not to this extent. I figured it would come back the next week. The next week, it dropped more. *Well, it'll still come back ... I hope.* The next week, it dropped yet again.

Ordinarily, I would have freaked out. Also, we would have informed the church and had a corporate family discussion about it. But I believed God was leading me to trust him and wait patiently — something diametrically opposite to my natural tendency to faithlessly seek control. So we simply took it before God in prayer. I sought him. And I didn't worry ... at all.

Now, in the past, as a Christian Atheist, I would have crawled into bed, curled up into the fetal position, and called for my mom. But this was different somehow. When we realized that the offerings were not returning to normal levels, we started paying salaries and expenses out of financial reserves. That was scary because, honestly, we do a lot of ministry, which means we have a lot of staff members. And they need to eat. And they have kids who need to eat. I feel personally responsible to these people who have chosen to be a part of our ministry.

I started asking God what he was trying to teach me. First, what was he asking me to do? I felt God was answering, "When you have proven faithful with little, I will trust you with much." I started doing what I could do. I began investigating where we might have been unfaithful with God's resources. Our church is a sizable organization. Our campuses are dispersed geographically, so I don't see some of them face-to-face very often. I got personally involved. I asked our key leaders to dig deep, to show me every place where we were investing our resources. And frankly, we found some sloppy expenditures.

Next we did what was wise. We made aggressive cuts. I told our staff bluntly, "I think God withdrew some of our giving because we haven't been as faithful as we should be. God won't honor poor stewardship, so we're going to fix it."

This pruning process took about eight weeks. During that time, I was constantly talking to God: "I trust you. No matter what, I trust you." I felt God reassuring me, "Once you get this fixed, I'll bless you again." During the ninth week, we made a short video for the staff in which I explained, "We've done what God asked us to do. We've tightened everything we could. And now, no matter what, we are going to trust God." We broadcast that video to all of our campuses on a Thursday. That very next weekend, the giving returned, right back up to where it had been before. In fact, it grew slightly, then stabilized over the following months and has remained consistent since — even through increasingly difficult financial times.

We did what God asked. We did what was wise. We did what we could do. Even though it wasn't easy, we handed everything we couldn't do over to God, and he took care of the rest. I'm genuinely thankful. God had allowed me to see his faithfulness through enough yesterdays to realize that he would be faithful in today, and that I didn't have to worry about tomorrow. I gave it over to God.

Who do we believe in more? Ourselves or God? Our actions and decisions will reflect that.

If God does what you think he should do, trust him. If God doesn't do what you think he should do, trust him. If you pray and believe God for a miracle and he does it, trust him. If your worst nightmare comes true, believe he is sovereign. Believe he is good.

In Matthew 6:33 – 34, Jesus says, "But seek first his kingdom and his righteousness, and all these things will be given to you as well. Therefore do not worry about tomorrow, for tomorrow will worry about itself. Each day has enough trouble of its own." God is outside of time. He has no beginning, and no end. That means he has no yesterday and no tomorrow. He just is. So for God, tomorrow is the same as today, same as yesterday. Was God in control yesterday? Undoubtedly, yes. Is God in control today? You know he is. Then he's in control tomorrow too.

Time is not an issue for him. He's already present in tomorrow. So no matter what happens, trust God.

Listen to his promise: "'I know the plans I have for you,' declares the LORD, 'plans to prosper you and not to harm you, plans to give you hope and a future'" (Jer. 29:11). Even if the future God chooses for you isn't the one you would choose, trust him.

It won't be easy, but once you've walked with God for enough days and experienced his faithfulness time and again, you could actually stop worrying. Besides, we don't need to, as Jesus assured us that our heavenly Father cares for us. Proverbs 3:5 – 6 says it this way: "Trust in the LORD with all your heart and lean not on your own understanding; in all your ways acknowledge him, and he will make your paths straight."

I don't know what you're worried about today, but I do know that worry distrusts the promises and the power of God. I believe in God, and I choose to live in a way that demonstrates my confidence in him.

After all, he is wise. He is willing. And he is able.

CHAPTER 9

When You Believe in God but Pursue Happiness at Any Cost

One Sunday at church after I had finished preaching, I bumped into Lisa and Amanda, faithful members of our church. They serve sacrificially, pray regularly, and give consistently. Most in the community would describe these women as strong Christians. As they were leaving, I asked how they were doing. My friends politely explained that they didn't want to be rude, but they had to leave right away to catch a movie. Always on the lookout for good movie recommendations, I asked what they were going to see. Lisa beamed as she said, "We're going to see *Wedding Crashers* ... again! It's one of the funniest movies I've ever seen!" Just thinking about it, they giggled and grabbed each other's hands, like a couple of giddy schoolgirls.

Suddenly they remembered that Craig is not "regular friend"; Craig is "pastor friend." The happy-happy giggle fest ended abruptly in a moment of awkward silence. Then Amanda added, "But you and Amy definitely shouldn't see it."

I was genuinely startled. "Why not?"

"Well," Lisa began sheepishly, choosing her words carefully, "You're a pastor. This movie has a lot of bad scenes. You shouldn't see that."

What? Hang on a minute!

Now you may be thinking, *You're right, Craig. What are you, five years old? Who are they to judge what's appropriate for you? You're a grown man! You've got six kids! I doubt Owen Wilson and Vince Vaughn can show you anything you haven't seen before.*

That's probably true, but it's not really the point. Let's rewind our scene. Lisa and Amanda are Christians active in our church, and they are headed out to see the hilarious, if somewhat raunchy, *Wedding Crashers* for the second time. I looked it up: "Rated R for sexual content/nudity and language." Is it just me, or is it odd for someone to believe that viewing a movie could be wrong for me because of my profession, but completely acceptable to other Christians, just because they don't preach on the weekends?

Of course, I have my own share of double standards. If something could make me happy, it is easy to believe that must be what God wants me to do.

The Pursuit of Happiness

While it is true that God wants to bless you and has great plans for you, we venture into extremely dangerous territory when we start to believe that God's ultimate plan for us is our happiness. As Christian Atheists, we can subtly believe in God and confidently pursue happiness at all costs.

This seemingly slight misunderstanding radically reverses our role with God's role. If we believe that God wants us happy above all else, rather than acknowledging that our role is to serve God, we wrongly believe that God exists to serve us. God becomes a means to our end: happiness. To the Christian Atheist, the holy God of the universe is quietly transformed into a cosmic soda machine. If we give enough money, or pray the right prayer, or live the right way, God must deliver and do what we ask. He is the one who exists to bring us earth's ultimate reward of uninterrupted happiness.

Think about the implications of this polluted theology: "I tried religion, but it didn't make me happy. I went to church and it didn't make my life any better. God didn't help me have a better life, so either he failed me or he's not real. Either way, I'm not interested."

Virtually every message our society sends reinforces our desire for a life of bliss. Turn on any talk show and you'll hear about how you should be happy. Browse at any bookstore, and you'll lose yourself in the self-help section. (When I typed in "happy" on amazon.com, I found 10,635 books with the word happy in the title.) It is not uncommon to hear this message preached in churches across the world: "God wants you to be happy and enjoy your life. You deserve more, bigger, better, and faster." We're bombarded with the message to bow down and worship the false God of happiness.

Pursuing happiness seems like the right thing to do. If we're happy, then everything is going right for us, right? The problem is, what *seems* right may not always *be* right. Proverbs 14:12 says, "There is a way that seems right to a man, but in the end it leads to death."

Like the donkey chasing the carrot, many pursue what they believe will satisfy, but it never does. Recently I had a conversation after church with a young woman who retraced a string of decisions that seemed right at the time. When Rachel met Mitch in a co-ed softball league, she thought he was exceptionally witty and cute. It seemed right to her to date him, even though he wasn't a Christian. When he continued to avoid the subject of marriage, she thought moving into his apartment with him would make him happy, so it seemed right. Although she knew she shouldn't have sex with him, since it made him happy and made her feel loved, she did what seemed right. When Rachel discovered she was pregnant, it seemed right that they should marry. With the birth of their new child, it seemed right to trade in their paid-for sedan and go into debt for a new SUV. Unhappy in their small apartment, it seemed like buying a home might make them happy. Last week, Mitch said he had never loved her and walked out, leaving Rachel broke, devastated, and alone with a new baby. Even though every decision seemed like it would lead to happiness, all of them led to one desperate and seemingly hopeless situation.

Happiness Is Not the Point

God doesn't want us to be happy.

I realize this may come across as narrow-minded, and it's totally at odds with the sermons our culture preaches at us 24/7. It also makes some of us squirm. But that's the point.

Sometimes what we *think* will make us happy is the opposite of what God wants for us. Remember, God is not fair and doesn't always say yes to all of our prayers. Fortunately, God wants something better — infinitely better — but we can't get to that until we understand the ways that here-and-now happiness doesn't fit God's desire for our lives.

First, God doesn't want us to be happy when it causes us to do something wrong or unwise. In God's plan, the end never justifies the means.

For example, my youngest child is five years old. Here is the rest of the story I promised earlier to tell you. Her name is Rebecca Joy, but we call her Joy, or JoJo for short. Recently we were at a friend's house for a party, and my buddy has a zip line in his back yard. But this is no ordinary zip line; this is a zip line on steroids. It is long and steep with no way to stop but to jump off, so we made a rule that a child must be fourteen or older to ride it.

By the end of the day, the parents had stopped paying close attention. Disobeying the rules, JoJo and her twelve-year-old partner in crime decided it was their time to fly. Her friend hoisted her high enough to grasp the handle, and off she shot. JoJo zipped across, squealing with joy, "Wheeeeeee!" My little Evel Knievel was grinning ear-to-ear, having the time of her life — right up until she smacked face-first into the tree. The loud *thud!* her tiny body made when she crashed into the tree was sickening. Her small frame dropped to the ground, limp. Blood covered her face as she lay unconscious. Thankfully, she woke up. She only had to endure two layers of stitches in her chin, and she made a quick and full recovery. But the point is clear: it doesn't matter how much she enjoyed the ride — she paid for it at the end.

So many of us go through life like JoJo on the zip line. *Whee!* we think, as we ride an unwise or sinful lifestyle. Sin can be pleasurable for a short period of time (see Heb. 11:25), but it always catches up to you. God doesn't want you happy when you're doing something wrong or unwise.

Wrong Beliefs Don't Make Life Right

Recently at a grocery store, I bumped into a guy I knew. I did his premarital counseling and officiated his wedding. Excited to see him, I immediately gave him a big hug and asked him about his family.

He explained that he and his wife had divorced, so I asked if he was comfortable telling me what happened. For the next few moments, he explained how his wife didn't make him happy, and he didn't make her happy. Since neither was happy with the other, they divorced.

When we believe our pursuit of happiness gives us license to sin, we become Christian Atheists. God never condones sin, no matter how happy it makes us, or seems to make us. We are experts at rationalizing, but there's no getting out of this first principle of godly happiness.

God also doesn't want us to be happy when our happiness is based on the things in this world. Last night I was watching TV, and I discovered that I can't be happy without an Ab-Cruncher, a 110-piece knife set, and a blanket with holes in it so I can put my arms through it. Now I know why I've been miserable. I've been innocently going through life wondering what was missing. This whole time it was a Snuggie.

Usually, without our knowing it, our pursuit of happiness through stuff is doomed to fail because it is based on a lie. Our actions confirm that a disturbing number of us truly believe this equation: better possessions + peaceful circumstances + thrilling experiences + the right relationships + the perfect appearance = happiness.

Many of us live as if we honestly believe this phony formula. Even if we deny it with our mouths, the way we spend our time, money, and thoughts leaves little doubt.

Our culture has conditioned us to believe that the things we don't have are the things that will make us happy — never mind that many of those things didn't even exist five years ago. We blindly chase whatever is newer, shinier, or faster.

We crave peaceful circumstances. If we don't like a job, a

boss, a salary, or a coworker, we move on. If a college class is too difficult, we drop it. If a commitment takes too much time or effort, we abandon it.

When we aren't chasing peace, we're looking for thrills. It could be our favorite hobby, sport, vacation, or weekend high. When one thrill fades, it's time to pursue the next one, whatever the cost.

Or we might live haunted in the romantic pursuit of that ever-elusive "true love." Blinded by stories about saving Buttercup from the evil Prince Humperdinck, or by the princess kissing the frog who turns out to be a handsome and wealthy prince, we wander through life craving that perfect "one." Instead of seeking to serve one another, we wrongly believe that there's one person out there who exists solely to make us happy.

If it's not the perfect person, then it's our looks. If we just looked a bit better, everything would be better. Thinner, taller, stronger — and no option is off the table. Diets, surgery, drugs, and tanning beds are simply tools we use to make us look perfect — to make us happy.

When we believe the things of this world will provide happiness, we're settling for a counterfeit. My wife sent me to the grocery store by myself once, which is a dangerous thing. When I walked through the automatic doors, I saw a large container of crab dip for only $4.99. Sensing a bargain, I quickly snatched two. After returning home and trying my prize, I spit it out before swallowing. The crab meat was an imitation.

God hates it when we pass up on the real life and settle for the false promises of this world.

More Than Happy

When we reach the final principle of godly happiness, we find a promise of unbelievable blessing. God doesn't want us to be happy because God wants us to be blessed. The Greek word *makarios* in Matthew chapter 5, also known as the Beatitudes, can be translated as "supremely blessed." In other words, God wants us to be more than happy. The happiness of this world is based on fickle happenings, but the blessings of God transcend the things this world offers. Scripture says in Psalm 112:1, "Blessed is the [one] who fears the LORD, who finds great delight in his commands." Another way of looking at it: "More than happy is the one who fears the Lord." The Bible never says, "Blessed is the one who does something wrong in the pursuit of happiness," or, "More than happy is the one who settles for cheap, worldly imitations."

A couple of years ago at our church, we spent a month studying what the Bible says about life and death. We interviewed Staci, a mom in her late thirties who had a brain tumor. The doctors told her she had very little time to live. Unfortunately, they were correct. I had the honor of helping officiate her funeral service. Staci's husband and two young daughters sat bravely on the front row. They shared stories, read poems, and played a recording of Staci singing one of the most beautiful praise songs I have ever heard.

There were enough tears shed to fill a small swimming pool — and rightly so. There was nothing happy about our human loss. But I can promise you, there wasn't a person in that church building who couldn't sense the presence of God. Even in our human sorrow, there was a peace that transcended our ability to understand. We were absolutely not happy, but we were undeniably blessed in the divine comfort of our holy God.

It's only when we manage to quiet the Christian Atheist in us and seek God and his kingdom over the empty and hollow things of this world that we can experience true and lasting blessing. And when we do, we'll gladly turn off the television, shut down the computer, walk out of the expensive store, and seek more of God. We'll let go of our materialistic grip on the things of this world and we'll realize that the peacemakers, and those who hunger and thirst for righteousness, the humble, and the broken are more than happy.

Max Lucado told a story about a fish in his book *When God Whispers Your Name*. My version is slightly different. Let's start with a question: do you think a fish would be happy on a sandy beach? (If you have to ask a fifth grader, I'm worried about you.) The obvious answer is, of course not. The fish's little gills would be slapping in and out like hands clapping, his body flopping end to end like a crazed acrobat.

Imagine we give our fish friend $100,000 in cold, hard, tax-free cash. Do you think Fishy would be happy now? Can you picture him still flapping and flopping? Suppose we give him a cold Corona and a *Playfish* magazine. Again, Fishy would not be happy. No matter what we give the fish on the beach, it won't satisfy him. There's nothing that could make that fish happy on the beach — because he isn't made for the beach. The sand is not his home. Anything apart from water will leave him wanting for the place for which he was created.

The same is true of us. We are not happy with the things of this world because we're not made for this world! We are strangers, aliens, foreigners on earth. We are made to dwell forever with our Lord in heaven. (See Phil. 3:20.) We will never discover lasting happiness in the temporary things of this world because we weren't made to live a temporary life. That's why we should lower our expectations of this place. Earth is not heaven. It was never meant to be. That's why no amount of money, new house, new living-room furniture, new kitchen appliances, new clothes, new hair, new baby, new vacation, new job, new income, new husband, or new *anything* will ever satisfy us, because we were not made for the things of this world.

As Psalm 97:12 says, "May all who are godly be happy in the LORD and praise his holy name!" (NLT). Real happiness is found only in the Lord, and when we find it we'll understand, perhaps for the first time, how blessed we really are.

CHAPTER 10

When You Believe in God but Trust More in Money

When I was a brand-new follower of Jesus still in college, I went to church with a few friends one cold Sunday morning. During one of the worship songs, I saw a lady a few seats over who, from all appearances, had a difficult life. Her face was attractive, but premature lines told part of her story. Her well-worn clothes implied that she probably lacked discretionary spending money. I didn't know how to explain it at the time, but I felt compassion for her that continued to grow. Deep down, I felt like God was nudging me to give her all the money I had on me. I told you earlier about my worry problem. Not having enough money has been a lifelong worry for me, and it was highlighted again in this moment. Being somewhat selfish, I thought to myself, *Is that my spiritual enemy tempting me to be generous? No, it must be God.* When I pried open my wallet, all I had was a five-dollar bill. My logical mind jumped in, *That's not enough money to make a difference in her life. It's only five dollars. Besides, that's the money I was going to spend on my lunch. And I'm hungry.*

As much as I tried to argue, the feeling simply wouldn't subside. *Give her all the money you have — even if it's only five dollars.* Not wanting to disappoint what I thought was God's quiet voice, I softly approached this woman, afraid I might appear to be a freak or a stalker.

"Ma'am," I said gently, "I know this is going to sound strange, but I think God wants me to give this to you. I know it's not much, but it's all I have."

She glanced down at my meager five dollars, and I couldn't help feeling embarrassed. Did I insult her? Would she feel humiliated? But her countenance dramatically changed. Her eyes beamed. She looked like she'd just won the lottery. She threw her hands up, smiled at the ceiling, and shouted, "Thank you, God! I love you so much!" Then she hugged me, tears streaming down her face.

I tried to just give her the bill and slip away, but she grabbed me. She explained that when she woke up earlier in the day, she desperately wanted to go to church to worship God, but as a single mom, she was out of money and wouldn't get paid until Tuesday. She had only enough gas in her car to get to church, but not enough to get home. Torn between going to church and staying home, she asked God what she should do. After a few minutes seeking God, she felt God led her to go to church and trust him. So she put her eight-year-old son in the car and drove to church, unsure how they would get home.

When I gave her the small token of money, she knew five dollars would provide enough gas for her to get home and then some. God had miraculously provided for her. I walked away in awe at God's goodness. Then I thought to myself, *But now what am I going to do for lunch?* When church was over, a friend invited me to lunch and said he was buying. Instead of my normal fifty-nine-cent tacos, my friend got me an eight-dollar hamburger. God is so good!

Fast-forward several years, and I had that same sense again — that God wanted me to give everything I had in my wallet. This time it was for an older man I saw standing alone by his broken-down, junker vehicle. When I opened my wallet, instead of a five-dollar bill, I had only a hundred-dollar bill. I thought, *It must be the devil temping me to be generous again.* I immediately entered serious negotiations with the voice I thought was God's.

Last time, with the single mom, I obeyed. This time, I didn't. That's right. Keeping the money, I ignored the voice and drove on by.

When it comes to money, it might be easy to trust God when the stakes are low. But when the stakes get high, it's tempting to trust in money.

In Money We Trust

There's a great irony in the country where I live. Printed across the back of an American dollar bill are the words, "In God We Trust." Yet for most of us, that motto is simply not true. We might *say* that we trust in God, but our actions show what's really going on. We Christian Atheists often give lip service to God, but in our everyday lives, we're tempted to trust, serve, and worship the very money on which that slogan is printed.

The words of Jesus in Luke 12:34 leave us no room to hide: "Wherever your treasure is, there your heart and thoughts will also be" (NLT). If you saw the way I lived for years, you'd probably conclude that I didn't treasure God. Sure, I tried to avoid pursuing my own happiness and pleasure, but my actions made it clear that I treasured the things of this world. And if my treasure was in this world, then it wasn't in the things that matter to God. For too long, I *said* I believed in God, but I trusted in money. Is that true for you?

Trusting in money generally sneaks up on us. Most of us believe (maybe secretly) that money can bring us happiness. Maybe you don't think that. Maybe like the Beatles, you believe that all you need is love. Let's try a little experiment and ask ourselves, Could even just a little more money make your life better? Most of us would say yes, with three exclamation points. The contradiction is convicting. Many of us say money won't bring happiness while we believe more really will.

Another way money slips in is that when we have "enough," we feel secure. Enough is different amounts for different people. I might require more than you do to feel secure. Or not. I remember one time when I was a kid, I sat on the porch with my grandma, and she told me stories about the Great Depression, horrors that she herself had lived through. Right then, during that conversation when I was eight years old,

I decided that I could never allow *my* family to go through anything like that. I vowed to myself that we'd always have enough money. My young mind made an unconscious choice to serve my functional savior — money. To me, more money always equaled more security.

The End of Our World?

For anyone who had placed their hope, happiness, and security in money, the closing months of 2008 provided a sobering wake-up call. You couldn't go anywhere without hearing people talking about the global financial meltdown. Even lifelong Christians, who should have been looking to God for their provision, found themselves panicking. The curtain was pulled back, and our false god of money was clearly revealed.

The reason money is such a struggle for so many of us is that it's clearly the number-one competitor for our hearts. First Timothy 6:10 says, "For the love of money is a root of all kinds of evil. Some people, eager for money, have wandered from the faith and pierced themselves with many griefs." Many people misquote this verse by saying "Money is the root of all evil." But money is not evil. Money is amoral. Money can be used for good or for evil. It is the *love* of money that is the root of all kinds of evil. Love of money leads to other abuses, whether of power, of sex, or other sins.

This issue is so important that even Jesus addressed it head-on: "No servant can serve two masters. Either he will hate the one and love the other, or he will be devoted to the one

and despise the other. You cannot serve both God and Money"
(Luke 16:13).

Sadly, the actions of many Christian Atheists indicate that
they worship money instead of God. Some even live as though
they believe that God exists to help us acquire more money
and things. In my opinion, this is the root of the dangerous
prosperity gospel. Although it's true that God wants his people
blessed, many believe that means that God wants everyone rich.
Anyone who has ever experienced deep, meaningful love in
relationships knows that you can be blessed in more than one
way. God isn't against people having money and things, but he
certainly hates when money and things have his people.

Two Encounters

Matthew tells two stories about rich guys who meet Jesus. The
first one is an intelligent, well-educated, rich young man whose
life is on the upswing. He probably graduated at the top of his
class, was promoted quickly, and became a wealthy leader.
When he meets Jesus, he asks him what he needs to do to have
eternal life. Jesus responds directly: "If you want to be perfect,
go, sell your possessions and give to the poor, and you will have
treasure in heaven. Then come, follow me" (Matt. 19:21).

Jesus challenged him to choose his master, and the next
verse reveals his response: "When the young man heard this, he
went away sad."

We might think we'd never reject Jesus like that, but many
of us make similar choices every day of our lives. We spend

more on coffee and music than we give to our church. We regret missing our favorite television show more than missing our Bible reading. We wake up in the morning dreaming of how we can make more money, rather than how to give more money.

After the young man had left, Jesus continued the conversation with his disciples: "I tell you the truth, it is hard for a rich man to enter the kingdom of heaven. Again I tell you, it is easier for a camel to go through the eye of a needle than for a rich man to enter the kingdom of God" (vv. 23–24).

For years, when I read that verse, I never applied it to myself. I didn't see myself as rich. You probably don't either. There's always someone richer. But instead of comparing ourselves with our neighbors, we need to compare ourselves with the rest of the world. More than half of the people on earth live on less than two dollars a day in conditions of incredible squalor and hardship. The reality is that most of us in North America are filthy rich. Unfortunately, Jesus shows that our wealth puts us at an extreme spiritual disadvantage.

We rich people have a hard time trusting God because we trust our money instead. You know that part of the Lord's Prayer, "Give us today our daily bread"? What does that really mean to us? Have you ever seen God provide for you miraculously? I personally have never missed a meal because I couldn't afford it or didn't have any food. Yet even though we're rich, most of us don't *feel* rich. And since we don't feel rich, we want more of the very thing that is crippling us spiritually. We're doubling down on the sickness instead of looking for the cure.

The other rich guy Jesus encountered wasn't nearly as moral as the first. His name was Zacchaeus. Now, Zacchaeus was a wee little man, and a wee little man was he. (That Sunday school song will haunt me for the rest of my life.) Zacchaeus was despised by everyone who knew him. He was a contractor, a tax collector for the Roman government, which in practice meant that he had an implied license to steal. Whatever he collected above what a person owed, he could keep for himself.

One day when Jesus came to town, Zacchaeus scrambled up into a tree. He wanted to see Jesus for himself, so he had to find a high vantage point that would let him see over the crowd. When Jesus looked up and saw Zacchaeus in the tree, he invited himself to Zacchaeus' house, a move that confused many people. Why would Jesus associate with such a well-known sinner? Jesus didn't ask Zacchaeus to sell his possessions or give any money to the poor, as he had asked the rich young ruler. However, Zacchaeus, with an instinctive spirit of repentance, said, "Look, Lord! Here and now I give half of my possessions to the poor, and if I have cheated anybody out of anything, I will pay back four times the amount" (Luke 19:8).

Zacchaeus' actions stated clearly how his heart had suddenly changed: "I was all about money — what it could buy and the security it provided. But when I truly saw and met Jesus, money no longer mattered to me at all."

Unlike the rich young ruler, this corrupt tax collector was so hungry for salvation and fellowship with Christ that he easily released his hold on worldly wealth to grab something far more valuable. "Jesus said to him, 'Today salvation has come to this house, because this man, too, is a son of Abraham. For the Son of Man came to seek and to save what was lost'" (vv. 9 – 10).

I understand Zacchaeus. His story is my story. Some days, the Christian Atheist in me forgets what's important. I focus on my job, on the people around me, the tasks I have to accomplish, the physical things my family needs. I have to first get really quiet, then give my total attention to God. I pray, worship him, thank him, and ask for his direction. I read his words in the Bible to hear him speak to me. When I don't remain focused on the things that are important to him, my heart drifts toward the things of this world instead — more and bigger, better, faster — most of all to my own selfish desires. But when I stay close to my God and savior, the temporary things in this world don't seem so shiny anymore. Because God is more than enough.

Putting Jesus first brings a strange contentedness. As Paul explained to Timothy, "Command those who are rich in this present world not to be arrogant nor to put their hope in wealth, which is so uncertain, but to put their hope in God, who richly provides us with everything for our enjoyment" (1 Tim. 6:17). People who lost everything they had saved for a lifetime in the stock market can tell you just how uncertain wealth is. But God not only wants to provide for us, he wants us to enjoy it.

If you don't believe this is true, here's your assignment: Purchase everything you can afford. Don't deny yourself anything you desire. Travel, accumulate, and store everything you've ever wanted. Make more money. Sacrifice your family if you must. Arrive at the end of your life and ask yourself honestly if all the things you had fulfilled you. I promise you that your answer will be a hard no. Sadly, this is the way many are already living — and dying.

Think back to the last possession that you really wanted, and then you finally purchased it. It felt good, didn't it? Does it still? What about the possession before that one? And before that one? The farther back you go, the less precious those things feel. Where does it end? It doesn't. Ecclesiastes 1:8 says, "The eye never has enough of seeing, nor the ear its fill of hearing." Next year's model is always waiting in the wings, ninety days same as cash — forever.

When we learn to trust in God alone, he is the one who provides us with what matters and lasts. Suddenly the earthly possessions that once gripped us don't hold us like they used to. Instead of seeing what we have as belonging to us, we see it as available to God for his use and his glory. And you get to play a really cool part in that story. Then we can follow the next piece of advice Paul offered Timothy: "Command them to do good, to be rich in good deeds, and to be generous and willing to share. In this way they will lay up treasure for themselves as a firm foundation for the coming age, so that they may take hold of the life that is truly life" (1 Tim. 6:18 – 19). Life that is truly life.

Enough Is Enough

I'm forty-two years old. For most of my adult life, I focused on becoming financially secure (whatever that means). When I was nineteen, I started buying small, inexpensive rental properties.

By the time I was twenty-eight, Amy and I sold all of our rental homes to pay off our primary home, and we still had money left over. Building on this foundation, we've always lived debt-free and beneath our means so we could save and invest for the future.

I always told myself, one day when we have a certain amount saved, then I'll feel secure. Yet each time I crossed that imaginary line of security, my line moved. What before seemed like more than enough suddenly didn't feel like close to enough.

After serious prayer and reflection, I realized what I was doing. I was placing my trust in money instead of in God. I talked to Amy about it, and she agreed. "We have enough. We have way more than enough. If we can't be happy with all that we have, there's something seriously wrong and sick about us." Here's what's surprising: it was easy to do. When my Christian Atheist let go of those false promises of worldly pleasures, it was easier for me to pursue God. And pursuing God, I became strangely content. That was enough.

When possessions no longer held us hostage, we saw what we had as being tools to use to help people and glorify God. Unfortunately, we were going directly against the grain of American — and even American Christian — culture. Americans are not known for being sacrificially generous. In fact, 21 percent of consistent American church members don't give *anything* to their church — not a single cent. Seventy-one percent of Christians give less than 2 percent of their income.

Yet the Bible is clear that Christians are called to give generously, lest they start trusting money until it becomes their god. The Old Testament teaches that we should return 10 percent to God. (See Mal. 3:10.) Some people argue against the tithe, claiming that it's only an Old Testament command. But looking to the New Testament, we find that Jesus affirmed the tithe. Some Pharisees were bragging about their tithe, and Jesus explained that they should not only tithe but also not neglect other important matters. Jesus said in Matthew 23:23, "You should tithe, yes, but you should not leave undone the more important things" (NLT).

Hearing that you should give a full 10 percent often induces involuntary seizures. "What!?" people exclaim, dumbfounded. "To give 10 percent would mean I'd have to totally rearrange my life!"

Exactly! You get to rearrange your life around God! Every day that we sacrifice something and honor God with our tithe reminds us that we're putting God first in our lives, even above our finances. Tithing forces us to have faith, and we get to be faithful in our giving.

The reality is that many wealthy Christian Atheists serve leftovers to a holy God. If they have a little left after buying everything their hearts desire, they toss some crumbs to God. We're not talking about making ends meet, or struggling to buy school clothes for the kids; we're talking about a bigger house, a third car, and a fourth television. We're talking about data plans, digital cable, and eating out for most meals.

You might think this is a new phenomenon. It's not. Some people in the Old Testament did the same thing. God told them to bring their best lambs to sacrifice. They did the same thing many of us would do today. They looked at their best, most prized lamb and thought, *This one's too valuable. It's gonna get sacrificed anyway. I'll just give a shabby one to God. He won't mind.* But he does care. God says in Malachi 1:8, "When you bring blind animals for sacrifice, is that not wrong? When you sacrifice crippled or diseased animals, is that not wrong? Try offering them to your governor! Would he be pleased with you? Would he accept you?" But the Christian Atheist justifies himself: *Sure, I'll give ... as long as it doesn't lower my standard of living.*

I lived that way for far too long. In essence, I gave comfortably and made sure it never took any real faith to give. So many people today want to give without sacrificing anything. King David was the opposite. A guy named Araunah offered David oxen and wood for an altar to sacrifice to the Lord. But David said, in 2 Samuel 24:24, "No, I insist on paying you for it. I will not sacrifice to the LORD my God burnt offerings that cost me nothing."

In other words, I want to feel it when I give.

Giving until It Hurts

Our family has agreed to increase the percentage of what we give each year. Instead of increasing our standard of living, we're increasing our standard of giving.

We decided to practice this at Christmas this year. We sat down with our kids and proposed a much different plan than their usual wish lists for the latest and best toys, games, and clothes. We asked the kids if they would consider not giving or receiving presents this year. Instead, we would give what we'd normally spend to support an orphanage. At first, they protested. "That's crazy!" Amy and I gently reminded them how much we have. We shared true stories about the horrid conditions of this orphanage in another country. After hearing about the children who have nothing, my six — who have almost everything — happily voted unanimously in favor of this decision. It was probably the best Christmas we've ever had.

This principle seems to come to my kids naturally. My daughter Anna had been saving her money faithfully to purchase a digital camera. She asked for odd jobs to make a few dollars to help her reach her goal. One afternoon as she and Amy leafed through some mail, they came across a request for money to purchase Bibles. It bothered Anna deeply that many people didn't have access to God's Word. When Anna continued to ask for jobs, we'd find something for her to do for an extra fifty cents or a dollar, assuming it would go toward her camera. After several more days, our ten-year-old brought us forty dollars in ones and change.

"I've decided other people need Bibles more than I need a camera. Would you send this money to help them get Bibles?"

"Anna, are you *sure* that's what you want to do with this?" I asked.

She smiled. "Of course, Dad. Isn't that what it means to be a Christian?"

I'm extraordinarily proud of her. And I'm trying to learn from her — and my wife.

While God is still working me over, Amy, on the other

hand, could give everything away and not worry a bit. Because she is so generous, we agree on a giving budget for her each year. She has total freedom to give wherever she wants. Each year for her birthday, she refuses presents and simply asks for an increase in her budget to give.

This year I felt God really speaking to my heart to substantially raise her giving budget. The amount in my mind caused me to panic and break out in a cold sweat. To give that much would take a lot of faith. With six kids, I've got plenty of braces, cars, colleges, and weddings to think about. I argued with God and said, "But God, if I let her give this much, I'd have to trust you with the future." As soon as I said it, I knew God had me cornered. It was 11:30 p.m. on Amy's birthday. With only thirty minutes left on her day, I gave in. I got out of bed, wrote a symbolic check, and presented it to her as her new giving budget. It was a holy moment.

The Joy of Sacrificial Giving

Along with her generous heart, another one of Amy's gifts is that she does whatever it takes to keep our family healthy. Unfortunately for me, she has transitioned us to a mostly vegetarian diet, which has left me feeling seriously meat deprived. I don't really care if red meat isn't good for me — it's good! The occasional steak or juicy cheeseburger makes me feel close to God. I know some guys who go out of town to drink beer or chase women. Not me. I sneak out to get a twelve-ounce sirloin.

Recently I traveled to Tegucigalpa, Honduras, with our

church to help build homes for people in need. Our translator took our leaders into the home of a single mom. To call it a home is really a gross overstatement; it was barely a shack, built mostly from cardboard. Five people lived in a space about the size of our master bedroom closet. It had dirt floors, no running water, and a hole in the back yard to take care of business. It was so dirty that it made me nervous when the sweet lady served us lunch.

With a warm smile and more hugs than I'm used to, she placed some form of meat in front of me. Not wanting to insult her, I ate the meatlike substance, praying with each bite for God's protection. When we finished our sparse meal, my translator asked if I noticed that no one else had meat.

Once he mentioned it, the truth hit me — every other plate had been covered with beans and tortillas. He explained that she had been told how much I like meat. Tears started to roll down my cheeks as he explained that she never enjoyed meat herself, and that she had saved her money for months to bless me with meat.

We Christian Atheists are slaves. This Honduran woman is truly free.

Why is it that those who have so little often seem to have so much? And why do those with so much seem to have so little that really matters? This woman who had nothing sacrificed to give a gift to a guy who had everything. Although she had none of the things we chase after every day, she had everything that we lack — peace, contentment, and true joy in the Lord.

I'd give all my money to be more like her.

CHAPTER 11

When You Believe in God but Don't Share Your Faith

YEARS AGO I RECEIVED A CALL FROM A CHURCH MEMBER explaining that her dad, Frank, was close to death. He occasionally attended our church with his daughter, but he did not believe in Christ and was skeptical of all pastors. His concerned daughter asked if I'd visit him in the hospital to explain the gospel so her dad would have a final chance to know Christ before he died.

Hospital visits have always made me uncomfortable. Some pastors seem to naturally know what to say. They hug everyone in the room, and after their visit, even a dire situation seems brighter. I'm much more awkward, and for better or for worse, I almost always say what I'm thinking. I've had to learn the hard way not to look at someone in a hospital bed and say, "Wow, you don't look so hot."

Walking down the long, sterile hallway, I glanced in each

room and wondered about the patients. Some would recover and go back to their lives, while others would never leave this building. When I reached Frank's room, I walked in nervously. His skin looked deathly yellow, as he lay on his bed. Even if God performed a miracle, Frank, age eighty-two, didn't have many years left to live. When he heard me enter the room, Frank stirred and seemed glad for a visitor, even if the visitor was a pastor.

Not wanting to come across like a typical fire and brimstone preacher, I kept the conversation light. The whole time we talked, I looked for the opportune moment to shift the conversation toward spiritual issues. We talked about his favorite football team. Frank loved the Redskins and hated the Cowboys ever since Tom Landry left. (No apparent opportunity for a spiritual segue.) He told me about his grandson, who is playing on the varsity baseball team as a sophomore. (No easy way to jump from baseball to Jesus.) We chatted about the unseasonably hot weather. (I considered mentioning the heat of hell, but thought better of it.)

The perfect moment to transition the conversation to a spiritual issue never came. I decided not to force it. I told myself that I'd developed a better relationship with him and would return the next day to try to talk to him about Christ and eternity.

The following morning as I walked back down that same bleak hallway, I tried to keep my dress shoes from clicking against the floor. I felt the familiar discomfort. When I turned the corner to enter his room, I couldn't see Frank because the room was packed with people. Instantly I realized what had just happened. Moments before I arrived, Frank had died, and all of his family had gathered to say goodbye. Standing outside the room, I could barely breathe. Frank's body may still have been warm, but my heart felt suddenly cold with disappointment in myself.

No one saw me, so I quickly turned around and walked back to my car, ashamed that I had missed a chance to impact Frank's eternity. I truly believe that Christ is the only door through which we enter heaven, but I failed to share him with a man at death's door.

Hesitant Witnesses

Many people can understand my hesitancy in sharing with Frank. People who are pushy about their beliefs aren't well-respected. The book *The Day America Told the Truth* tells how Americans ranked different professions according to their degree of integrity and honesty. Televangelists, known mostly for asking for money, ranked below lawyers, politicians, car salesmen, and even prostitutes. Out of seventy-three professions, only organized crime members and drug dealers scored lower than televangelists.

The word *evangelism* comes from the Greek word *euangelizo*, which means "to proclaim or share the good news." Our modern word *gospel* comes from the Old English word *gôdspel*. In Old English, *gôd* with a long "o" meant "good," and *spell* meant "word." So sharing the gospel meant sharing the good word or good news of Christ.

Yet for those who don't believe in Christ, gospel sharing, or evangelism, often arouses skepticism, resentment, fear, or anger. For many self-proclaimed Christians, these words often induce feelings of fear and guilt. As my experience with Frank illustrates, Christian Atheists know they should share their faith, but largely because of the strong emotions associated with it, they usually don't.

During my first year of seminary, I took a class on evangelism at Southwestern Baptist Theological University. I have only two memories from that class. The first was that we had to memorize a gospel-sharing script to recite to our victims. I can still remember the opening line: "Have you come to a place in your life that if you died tonight, you're certain you'd spend eternity in heaven?"

Nice icebreaker, huh?

The second thing I remember was the professor telling us that we should always pray before knocking on someone's door. As a class requirement, we went out door-to-door to witness to total strangers (while our instructor listened and graded us on our presentation). I was incredibly intimidated by what felt to me like a forced spiritual invasion. But I did one part of the assignment very well — I prayed outside every home. Often, with all the faith I could muster, I pleaded, "Dear God in heaven, don't let anyone be home!"

Why are so many of us Christian Atheists slow to share our faith? There are many possible answers, among them the strong desire not to be pushy or disliked. Also, many don't feel they know enough. And the list could go on, but I believe one of the main reasons people don't share their faith in Christ is that they don't really believe in hell. Many of us are out of touch with the genuine urgency.

As a pastor, I'm often confronted by death. One thing I've observed is that when someone dies, that person's loved ones want to believe their relative went to "a better place." We'll say things like, "She wasn't a religious person, but deep down, she had a good heart," or, "He wasn't a saint, but he did some good things." When it comes to death and eternity, it's human nature to hope for the best and avoid contemplating the worst.

Research shows that while almost three out of four people believe in heaven, less than half believe in hell. Think about the ramifications: if hell didn't exist, unbelievers would easily reject Christ with no fear of God whatsoever, and believers would be unmotivated to share their faith in Christ with nonbelievers.

But opinion polls don't determine reality. God has created a universe with a heaven — and a hell. He's told us about both. And Christians take these truths to heart. We are here to help others come to terms with reality. Are we living as lights in a dark world? Be honest. When was the last time you were so burdened for someone far from God that you spent the whole day or night praying on their behalf? How many people have you brought with you to church to hear the gospel this past month? When was the last time you had a non-Christian in your home? (The plumber repairing your leaky faucet doesn't count.) Is there someone in your family who doesn't know

Christ? How about an old friend, a neighbor, or someone at work?

If we really believed in heaven and hell — and we sincerely cared — wouldn't our actions be transformed?

Endless Suffering

If we truly understood what hell was like, we'd be much more motivated to help people avoid going there. Hell is a place of unspeakable suffering. Jesus says in Matthew 5:29, "If your right eye causes you to sin, gouge it out and throw it away. It is better for you to lose one part of your body than for your whole body to be thrown into hell." Can you imagine gouging out your own eye? According to Jesus himself, as horrible as it would be, digging your eye out would be far better than being punished for your sins in hell.

In Revelation 14:10 – 11, an angel speaks about those who will worship the beast. It says that they "will drink of the wine of God's fury, which has been poured full strength into the cup of his wrath. He will be tormented with burning sulfur in the presence of the holy angels and of the Lamb. And the smoke of their torment rises forever and ever. There is no rest day or night for those who worship the beast and his image, or for anyone who receives the mark of his name." Those verses are difficult to read. They're even more difficult to imagine. The Bible calls hell a fiery furnace, a place of burning sulfur, the outer darkness, and a place where there is weeping and gnashing of teeth.

For those who don't understand hell, it's easy to joke around. "If I'm going to go to hell, at least there will be a lot of company there. I'll hang out with my buddies and have some fun." That couldn't be farther from the truth. In hell, there will be complete separation from God and people. How do you punish the worst of criminals? You put them in solitary confinement and isolate them. Imagine the physical pain of endless suffering, the emotional void of hurting without anyone to comfort you, and the knowledge that you'll suffer alone with no relief coming — ever.

Heaven Can Wait

No one I know wants to go to hell. That's understandable. It's interesting to me, though, that not many people want to go to heaven — at least not anytime soon.

The reason most prefer to postpone eternity in heaven is because we simply don't understand what heaven will be like. Many people I talk to think heaven will be like a really long church service. In reality, nothing could be farther from the truth. The psalmist said in Psalm 84:10, "Better is one day in your courts than a thousand elsewhere." Can you imagine? Pick your ten favorite moments from this life. You land your dream job. You travel to your most desired vacation spot. You meet the love of your life. You watch your first child being born. You push your grandchild on a swing. And yet one day with God is better than a lifetime of your favorite moments.

If you enjoy your life now, imagine life without any sin,

sickness, death, mourning, or pain. The Bible says in Revelation 21:4 – 5, " 'He will wipe every tear from their eyes. There will be no more death or mourning or crying or pain, for the old order of things has passed away.' He who was seated on the throne said, 'I am making everything new!' "

In heaven, we will actually dwell with God. Revelation 21:3 says, "Now the dwelling of God is with men, and he will live with them. They will be his people, and God himself will be with them and be their God." The lyrics to the song "Amazing Grace" will be more true than we could imagine: "When we've been there ten thousand years / Bright shining as the sun / We've no less days to sing God's praise / Than when we'd first begun."

Intellectually I believe in both heaven and hell. But practically — the way I live daily — doesn't reflect the urgency of my claimed beliefs. If eternity were at the front of my mind, I'd pray far more for those distant from God. I'd share my faith in Christ on a daily basis. I'd serve my way into people's lives. Instead of accumulating more and more, I'd use everything I have to spread the gospel around the world. If I really believed, my life would look much different than it does.

The challenge is that many believe heaven is the default destination when, in fact, the opposite is true. Jesus told us to "enter through the narrow gate. For wide is the gate and broad is the road that leads to destruction, and many enter through it. But small is the gate and narrow the road that leads to life, and only a few find it" (Matt. 7:13 – 14). If we embraced the reality that many are traveling toward an eternal hell and few are on the road to eternal life, don't you think we'd overcome some of our Christian Atheism and reach out to those who are walking on the broad path?

Always Be Ready

Once, I was with a few Christian friends on the El in Chicago, and we were chatting about Jesus. A young man politely interrupted us and explained that he couldn't help overhearing our conversation. He asked if we were Christians. On behalf of the group, I explained that we were.

His eyes brightened. "I've been searching for a while, and I don't know what I believe," he said with sincerity. "Can you tell me exactly what it means to be a Christian and how I can become one?"

A hunter would say, "This guy's a sitting duck." If you're playing basketball, "It's a slam dunk." If you're taking a test, "This one's a no-brainer." In other words, you couldn't find an easier guy to lead to the Lord — unless, like us, you were unprepared.

Stunned by his straightforward question, I hesitated. *Wow. Where should I start?* My mind flashed back to my seminary class. Reciting to him the opening line of the script from my evangelism class certainly didn't feel like the best way to go. I remembered another witnessing technique called the "Four Spiritual Laws," but a canned presentation to his heartfelt question didn't seem right. As my mind raced, I couldn't figure out what to say, so I just started talking, hoping I'd make sense.

The confused look on the man's face told me I wasn't. Shifting gears, I decided to tell him how I became a Christian. Several minutes into my story, he interrupted me to explain he had to get off the train at the next stop. Not sure what to say in the last minute or so, I stuttered and stammered awkwardly. When the sliding doors opened, he stood and looked at me before politely speaking words I'll never forget.

"Oh well, thanks for trying."

He stepped off the train, and I watched the doors slide shut.

The apostle Peter says, "Always be prepared to give an answer to everyone who asks you to give the reason for the hope that you have" (1 Peter 3:15). Maybe you can relate. You'd like to be ready for anything, but you're afraid you might choke under pressure. Preparation — studying and thinking about what you'll say — will give you confidence.

Not every chance to share will be set up for you as obviously as it was for me on that train. You'll recognize some opportunities — clearly presented to you by God — in which you are called to take the initiative. But no matter who starts the conversation, if you engage enough people, you're going to be amazed how many of them are genuinely hungry to hear the truth from an honest, caring heart.

Invite Someone to Church

There are several New Testament examples of unlikely evangelists that may provide you with the confidence to share your faith whenever God gives you an opportunity. Our first unlikely witness had a couple of major strikes against her. First, she was a woman. During the time Jesus lived, most men didn't treat women with the respect or dignity they deserved. Second, she'd already been through five husbands and was living with a sixth guy. Yet God used this unlikely person to reach out to many with the love of Christ.

When this woman met Jesus at a well, she noticed that he treated her differently. She was shocked, in part, because a Jew (probably also a religious teacher, by his traditional dress) wouldn't normally speak to a Samaritan, much less treat her kindly. As they continued talking, Jesus cleverly turned the conversation about water from a well to a conversation about living water. He promised her that if she had this living water, she'd never thirst again.

Overwhelmed by his love and grace, the changed woman had to tell everyone she knew. John 4:28 – 30 says, "Then, leaving her water jar, the woman went back to the town and said to the people, 'Come, see a man who told me everything I ever did. Could this be the Christ?' They came out of the town and made their way toward him."

Even though this forgiven woman hadn't memorized the script I learned in seminary, even though she wasn't a great defender of her faith, able to debate skeptics, and even though she probably didn't know much about Scripture, she could invite her friends to experience Jesus. Later in the chapter, we see the great results from her efforts: "Many of the Samaritans from that town believed in him because of the woman's testimony" (John 4:39).

You can make a similar difference in people's lives with a simple invitation. You can invite someone to church, to your Bible study, or to your church softball team. You can bring someone along to a Christian movie, concert, or production. Even though you may not know what to say, you can invite people to places where they might hear about the good news of Christ or experience his love through his people.

One weekend when I wasn't preaching, one of our campus pastors, a young, bald-headed guy with a goatee, spoke in my place. The next week, I was at a movie-rental store when I heard a lady inviting a friend to church. Curious, I crept a little closer to eavesdrop on their conversation. The first lady said, "I'm not a religious person or anything, but you have to try this church called Life Church. It's incredible. It totally changed my life." I was blessed to overhear a conversation of someone who'd been touched by God at the church I pastor.

Unfortunately the lady must have noticed me listening in. She looked straight at me and said, "Hey you, you need to come to church with me too. The preacher is amazing." Still excited but slightly confused, I asked her what the preacher looked like, confident she'd recognize me at any moment. Still talking fast, she said, "He's bald and has a goatee." This lady who had been to our church only one time was inviting everyone she saw — even me — the pastor of the church.

You can do the same thing. Take a step of faith and invite someone to go with you where they will hear about God's love through Christ.

Share Your Faith Story

We looked briefly in an earlier chapter at a guy who was born blind. After Jesus healed him, others in his town who didn't understand wanted to debate all sorts of meaningless issues. When several Pharisees accused Jesus of being a sinner, the blind guy told his story: "Whether [Jesus] is a sinner or not, I don't know. One thing I do know. I was blind but now I see!" (John 9:25).

Even though this newly healed man didn't know enough to debate theology, he was an expert on one topic — his own experience. He was blind and now he could see. Everywhere he went, this healed man could tell his story to anyone who would listen, and his changed life was proof of what had happened.

We can do the same. Start with these words: "Let me tell you my story." Then just fill in the blanks. You might have been forgiven of many sins or saved from a life of drug addiction. Perhaps you were sick and God healed you, or you were searching for something meaningful in life and your search ended when you found Christ. You may have grown up in church and known about God since Elmo was your favorite furry friend, but you only personally experienced his goodness later in life. Even if you don't feel like your story is powerful or dramatic, God can use it.

Now, you might be thinking, *Yeah, but your personal story didn't work on the train, did it?* That's because I wasn't prepared. I knew my story, but I hadn't put any effort into planning how I would share it with someone else. You can prepare by writing your story out, or recording it, or practicing in front of a mirror or with another Christian. Then watch what God does with this tool that belongs to you alone.

You can write about your faith journey in a paper for a class in school. You could weave your testimony into a conversation with your boss. If you're an artist, you can paint a picture that illustrates what God did in your life. If you're into poetry, you can bring your story to life in a few stanzas. You can post your favorite Christian song to your Facebook status update. You can Twitter what God's doing in your life now in 140 characters or less. However you normally communicate, you can naturally weave in your own story.

Give Your Life Away

If you're a person who isn't as comfortable with words, you can show Christ with your actions. There's a brief story of a serving hero found in Acts: "There was a disciple named Tabitha (which, when translated, is Dorcas), who was always doing good and helping the poor" (Acts 9:36).

When Tabitha (which sounds so much better than Dorcas) lived, the law said that when a husband died, all his property went to his son. If the son who inherited his father's possessions didn't care for his mom, the widow, then she was in great trouble. The widows in her day were totally dependent on a man with an income or on the generosity of others. Tabitha devoted her life to caring for such widows who had been left to fend for themselves. I love the description of her ministry: "She was always doing good."

We can do the same thing. My friend, Matthew Barnett, pastors a church in a rough part of Los Angeles. Surrounded by crack dealers and prostitutes, he decided there was only one way to break into the lives of the broken people around him. He and a crew of passionate believers decided they'd love and serve their community as a way to share God's love.

Armed with tools and cleaning supplies, this band of Christian do-gooders walked from door to door asking how they could serve the people. Even though almost everyone was standoffish at first, Matthew and his friends promised to return each Saturday prepared to work. And work they did. Each week they knocked on doors offering to paint, clean, or do repairs. Before long they started developing friendships. When people realized these Christians were coming to help with no strings attached, their hearts began to soften. Over time relationships deepened, and now this church has seen hundreds of people set free from the bondage of both sin and poverty. When we serve in love, our lives look like Christ's life to the watching world.

It's amazing what a difference the little things will make. For example, years ago when I was a new believer, I always wore a tiny cross pin on my shirts. Because they were an inexpensive way to witness, I'd purchase a dozen or so at a time. Every time someone commented on mine, I'd give it to them as a gift. Once in a 7-11 convenience store, the female clerk complimented my cross pin. Instinctively I offered it to her. For several moments she tried to refuse, finally reluctantly accepting the small gift.

Years went by, and I'd almost forgotten about the 7-11 woman. After church one week, a woman stopped me in the lobby and said she had to thank me. Trembling as she spoke, she explained, "You probably don't remember me, but years ago you gave me this." She reached into her purse and pulled out the small cross pin. "When you offered me this cross, my life couldn't have been any worse. I didn't feel worthy of such a generous gift. But God showed me that he still loved me. My life is different today because of what you did for me."

What I did was almost nothing. But to someone else it meant almost everything. You don't have to be a Bible scholar to take some time to serve. You can clean someone's house, make a meal, mow a yard, watch someone's kids, or help with a garage sale. When you serve others in Christ's name, with no strings attached, people will notice something is different about you.

Be Bold with the Truth

You can be a witness in many different ways. You can invite people to church, share your story, or simply serve your neighbors. At times, however, God might lead you to get in someone's face and boldly confront them with truth.

Peter called it like he saw it. Instead of choosing his words with tact, he was more of a "ready, fire, aim" type of guy. He often acted before thinking. Whether he was arguing with Jesus about why Jesus shouldn't die, hopping out of a boat to walk on water, or swinging a sword at a temple servant's head, Peter never lacked for action.

Like Peter, you might naturally be more confrontational in your personality. Even if it's not natural to you, you might sense God giving you the courage to confront someone at a specific time. God's Holy Spirit landed on Peter at Pentecost, and he preached boldly, "'Repent and be baptized, every one of you, in the name of Jesus Christ for the forgiveness of your sins. And you will receive the gift of the Holy Spirit....' With many other words he warned them; and he pleaded with them, 'Save yourselves from this corrupt generation'" (Acts 2:38 – 40). That's not what we'd call "feel good" preaching, yet as a result of Peter's prophetic boldness, three thousand people were saved and baptized in one day.

You might have a close friend who is always reading the latest self-help book but never looking to the One who can help. Maybe it is time to lovingly confront your friend. Perhaps you're having coffee with a coworker who doesn't believe in God but doesn't know why. Could it be your role to ask some hard questions? Maybe a mom from your play group wonders why you seem to have a peace she doesn't have. Maybe God wants you to tell her the real reason instead of playing it safe. Don't be afraid to tell the truth in love.

One Day You Will Know

I once visited a man named Mark in the hospital. Like Frank, Mark was not a believer in Christ, and he didn't have much time to live. At the tender age of forty-two, this husband and father of two had an advanced brain tumor.

When I walked in, Mark recognized me. He was obviously in pain, and he didn't look thrilled at my visit. "My wife sent you, didn't she, Preacher?" he said cuttingly.

"As a matter of fact, she did," I replied. I was saddened that the conversation was already headed in an awkward direction. Mark had come to our church exactly twice — once to see his daughter baptized, and once to a Christmas Eve service to satisfy his wife.

"I guess you came to 'save' me from hell," Mark said, obviously positioning himself for a verbal conflict. My mind raced. What should I say? Should I play it down? Should I answer truthfully?

"Mark, that's exactly why I'm here," I said, holding my breath and praying for God's guidance. "Your wife loves you more than you know, and frankly, she's concerned for you spiritually. She's tried to talk to you about Christ, but you always shut her down. She thought you might be willing to talk to me."

Mark wasn't rude, but he was firm. "I don't have long to live. I don't want to waste a minute of what's left of my life talking about religion." He grimaced in pain. "If you don't mind, please shut the door on the way out so I can rest in peace."

Not wanting to be pushy, I politely excused myself.

As I walked down the hospital hallway, my mind flashed back to Frank. Overwhelmed with sudden spiritual courage, I turned. I charged back into his room, and with tears in my eyes I blurted out, "You know what, Mark? That's exactly what your family wants for you. They want you to rest in peace — eternally."

Mark didn't speak. For several awkward moments, we simply stared at each other. I didn't know what else to say. He too seemed at a loss for words. I could have counted to two thousand in those moments of silence. Finally, Mark was the first to gather himself. His face softened slightly and he said, "Well?"

Seeing a crack in the door, I tried to open it and show him God's good news. I began explaining to him how God sent his Son Jesus as a sacrifice for our sins. Soon I realized I hadn't taken a breath, so I paused and asked hopefully, "Mark, would you like to trust Jesus with your eternity?"

Mark didn't speak. He nodded his head gently, affirmatively.

We prayed together. I said the words and he repeated them. Moments later, I left.

Two days later I went back. Mark's wife was sitting by the side of the bed, holding her husband's hand. Although she was about to lose her husband, she beamed with assurance that she and her husband would be reunited in heaven. Though closer to death than ever, Mark's eyes looked more alive than a healthy man's.

"Preacher," he said, affectionately this time, "God has forgiven me of all my sins." Mark pushed his next words out slowly: "I'm going to see my family again in heaven one day." He seemed deeply satisfied.

Mark held his wife's hand with one hand, and he reached

out to me with the other. I stepped forward and took it. He said, "You'll never know what a difference you've made in my life."

I smiled and hugged him. The three of us chatted pleasantly for several minutes. As I left that day I thought, *Mark will never know what a difference he made in mine.*

When we are open to go wherever the Holy Spirit leads us, he will use us to share the greatest gift of all — eternal life through Christ. And when he does, we may never know on this side of eternity how much of a difference we made.

But someday — on the other side — we'll know in full.

CHAPTER 12

When You Believe in God but Not in His Church

I was sitting in a restaurant with my wife when our waiter, Brad, returned with Amy's salad and my cheeseburger. Moments after Brad left us to check on his other tables, we bowed our heads and quietly thanked God for our meal. We had barely finished when Brad returned to our table. He had seen us praying and asked enthusiastically, "Are you guys Christians?"

When we told him we were, he positively spilled all that Christ had done for him. Excited by his passion, I asked Brad what church he was a part of. Brad replied, "Oh, I don't go to church. Organized religion doesn't work for me."

I was intrigued. "Really? But you seem so excited about your faith. Why aren't you in a church?"

He glanced around to make sure no one else was listening, then leaned in closer. "Because the churches I've been to are

so far from what I read about in Scripture — I think I can be
a better Christian *without* the church than I can *with* the
church."

Church Isn't for Me

Christians from all denominations and walks of life shun the
church these days. Many believe they simply don't have time
for it. In years past, Sunday morning meant church, followed by
rest. But in our 24/7 world, Sunday is now just another weekday.
Most stores and restaurants are open. Our kids' sporting events
are in full swing. For some, Sunday is even a workday. For
others, Sunday is the only day they can sleep in or do chores
around the house. With so much going on, church has become
a lower priority.

Some people feel they have plenty of time for church. They
just don't *want* to go. Church repulses them because they feel
it's full of hypocrites. Who wants to hang out with a bunch of
people who claim to believe in something, then live differently
the rest of the week? Who hasn't known some church member
who always talks about God then is caught having an affair or
doing some other immoral act?

Other people accept that people are hypocrites by nature;
they just can't stand churches talking about money. To them
it seems like the pastor is always begging for money — even if
people don't have enough for themselves. They wonder how
churches plan to use all that money to truly make a difference.

Even if they can get past those issues, still others steer clear because church is irrelevant to their everyday lives. They tried church before, and it didn't make a difference. Why bother?

Maybe they even *want* to attend church, but when they do, they feel even guiltier than they did before. The pastor and all the other put-together, perfect people just make them feel worse about themselves.

Finally, people I call "superspiritual" know just what church should be like. But their ideals are so high that no church can possibly meet their standards. They have detailed lists of what's wrong with each church in town. The worship music isn't "Spirit-led" enough, or it's too loud, too soft, or too whatever. The sermons are too shallow or too intellectual. The missions program isn't aggressive enough or it's all the church talks about. They spend too much money on the building or not enough. Churches, with their mere mortals, can never measure up.

Who needs church anyway? We can get all the Christian content we need from websites, podcasts, and books — even television and radio. Pouring time, energy, and money into that weekly commitment is just a ritual that needlessly complicates our lives even more. It makes sense that non-Christians don't think about church. But even many Christians aren't asking, "Which church should I go to?" Instead, they're asking, "Why should I bother with church at all?"

Don't Go, Be

To many people, church is a place. It's a building, bricks and mortar, a destination. We *go to* church. The problem with thinking "we go to church" is that it gives us a consumer mindset: *I'm looking for a church that meets my needs. I need a good church that will help me.* The church is actually God's chosen vehicle to meet — through other human beings — people's true needs (including our own).

An expert in Hebrew law once asked Jesus, "What's the most important commandment?"

Jesus said essentially, "First, love God. Second, love other people as much as you love yourself. If you can do just these two things, that will fulfill every other law" (see Matt. 22:36 – 40). Church allows you to do both; it's where we can give ourselves to God by giving ourselves to others. Pastor and author Erwin McManus once said, "The church does not exist for us. We are the church, and we exist for the world."

Christian Atheists believe in God but not in his church because they think they don't need it. I once saw a church sign that read, "COME TO CHRCH! WHAT'S MISSING? U."

Have you ever considered, What if church really does need you?

In 1 Corinthians 12:12 – 27, the apostle Paul describes the church as a body, made up of different parts and organs. He calls us hands, feet, ears, and eyes. Paul explains that we should have "equal concern for each other." He says we are each indispensable. In Romans 12:4 – 8, Paul uses the body example again, focusing on how each part serves a different function. Have you ever tried to see with your ears? Or walk with your eyes? If I'm using my gifts in church, and if I don't do what I was made to do, then the whole body suffers as a result. Galatians 6:10 says, "Let us do good to all people, especially to those who belong to the family of believers." The "family of believers" is *our* family, the church. And the church needs me, whether I feel like I need it or not.

My mentor and friend Bill Hybels once said, "The local church is the hope of the world." Since Jesus lives in believers, we represent him to the world. We in the church are his hands and feet. *We're* God's plan to spread his good news — news of love, grace, forgiveness, and changed lives — to the entire world. Together, we can make a bigger difference than anyone ever dreamed possible. Ephesians 3:20 reminds us that we serve a God who "is able to do immeasurably more than all we ask or imagine, according to his power that is at work within us." Each believer has a gift and a role in the church and in the world. Isaiah 64:8 says, "LORD, you are our Father. We are the clay, you are the potter; we are all the work of your hand." No believer is so broken that the Master Potter can't put you back together. If you're not ministering and using your gifts in the church, then something God wants done is being ignored.

If you went to church and didn't like it — whether because you felt hurt, disillusioned, or disappointed — then be the change you want to see. Even though the church is far from perfect (mine sure is), think how much better it could be if you would give your life to it. God is not calling us to *go* to church; he is calling us to *be* his church, the hope of the world.

Extreme Church

Many Christian Atheists today commit only halfheartedly
to Christ's church — if at all. He doesn't want us simply to
believe in God. He wants us to give our lives to him through
his church. In the first church described in Acts 2, "church"
wasn't something people added to their lives. Church was the
center of their lives. Church was not a physical building; it
was the community of people who shared a belief and faith in
Christ. Their extreme commitment to Christianity contrasts
sharply with our attitude today: "They devoted themselves to
the apostles' teaching and to the fellowship, to the breaking of
bread and to prayer" (Acts 2:42). They didn't *go to* church; they
were the church, devoted to God's Word, God's people, and
God's mission.

The author of Acts continues, "Everyone was filled with
awe, and many wonders and miraculous signs were done by the
apostles" (v. 43). Imagine if you gave your life to Christ through
the local church and became so filled with God that everyone
noticed the difference. Imagine if your church was so involved
in the inner city that local government officials took notice.
Imagine if your church visited people in prison so regularly that
countless inmates became believers. Imagine if your church
prayed for all those sick in the hospital and sent prayer cards
to their families. Imagine what's possible if we stop going to
church and start being the church!

In one of the most beautiful images we have of Christ's
church, the early Christians made extreme sacrifices to become

a genuine family in truly practical ways: "There were no needy persons among them. For from time to time those who owned lands or houses sold them, brought the money from the sales and put it at the apostles' feet, and it was distributed to anyone as he had need" (Acts 4:34 – 35). This is what happens when people stop *going to* church and start *being* the church, as Jesus intended. Every need *in* the church can be met *by* the church.

One weekend at our church, I asked if anyone could volunteer to help elderly members repair their homes. Numerous hands shot up. I asked if anyone would drive a person who didn't have transportation to church each week. Again, many volunteered. I asked if someone would babysit kids to relieve a single parent for an evening. More people responded. I even asked who would donate an older car to someone in need. Each time I asked a question about sacrificial service, people responded. And together we started impacting tons of lives. That's what it means to *be* the church.

A Place to Belong

While the church meets physical needs, it also provides a place for us to belong. A Barna poll revealed that 92 percent of Americans claim to be independent. Though independence is a goal for many, God never intended for his believers to be independent. He wants us dependent on one another and on him. The apostle Paul writes, "So in Christ we who are many form one body, and each member belongs to all the others" (Rom. 12:5). As believers in Christ, we are incomplete without the rest of his body — the church. And the church is incomplete without us. We need others, and others need us.

All of us are looking for a place to belong. We belong to book clubs, gyms, sororities, gangs, choirs, moms' groups, and sports teams. But when a believer joins other Christians to do life together and to serve one another with no strings attached, their shared relationships are much deeper and more meaningful. When they were being persecuted by the Roman state, first-century Christians used the symbol of a fish (known as an *ichthus*) to identify one another or to mark secret meeting places. A Christian who met a total stranger who also followed Christ would have an instant bond: *We belong to the same spiritual family.* Just like Michelle, the girl on the plane, felt an immediate bond with me because of Christ, so should we with other Christians. When we as believers are committed to Christian fellowship, we are known and needed. We each have certain gifts and roles to play. Without us, the church is incomplete. When we use our God-given gifts in relationship with fellow Christians, we experience the deep satisfaction of being a part of the larger body of Christ.

Belonging to a local church also provides accountability, where wiser and more mature Christians can regularly counsel us, mentor us, comfort us, and help us heal. We can confess to God for forgiveness (see 1 John 1:9), but that's only half of the equation. We also need to confess to other Christians to help us ultimately overcome our sinful habits. James 5:16 says, "Therefore confess your sins to each other and pray for each other so that you may be healed."

When we hit relational bumps with others, instead of walking away and leaving the church, we can stay and work through our problems, which can help us grow spiritually as we learn to forgive.

In Matthew 18:15 – 17, Jesus lays out these practical guidelines: "If your brother sins against you, go and show him his fault, just between the two of you. If he listens to you, you have won your brother over. But if he will not listen, take one or two others along, so that 'every matter may be established by the testimony of two or three witnesses.' If he refuses to listen to them, tell it to the church." Jesus clearly assumes we'll all be together, connected and involved with the church. (Hint: that's why he says "the church.") And if we can be honest, sometimes it's *we* who need others' forgiveness.

According to Hebrews 10:24, we're responsible both to hold each other accountable and to encourage one another: "Spur one another on toward love and good deeds." Verse 25 tells us how: "Let us not give up meeting together, as some are in the habit of doing." Do you know someone who's "out of the habit" of meeting together? Are you? Verse 25 even tells us why it's important: "Encourage one another." We're not supposed to do life alone.

A Place to Believe

In addition to belonging, church also gives us a place to grow spiritually. Romans 10:17 says, "Faith comes from hearing the message, and the message is heard through the word of Christ."

Our faith grows as we hear God's Word taught and proclaimed. Living out what we've heard solidifies it for us. James 1:22 says, "Do not merely listen to the word, and so deceive yourselves. Do what it says."

Recently I was teaching at a church and — right in the middle of the talk — God prompted me to share something I hadn't planned. Without even knowing why, I heard myself say, "Someone here has decided today to walk away from Christ because there are so many things you don't understand. Keep believing in Christ." I went on to explain some things we can hold onto in our faith when everything around us is confusing.

After the service, a hip twenty-something approached me. With tears in his eyes, he told me that earlier in the day he had told God he was done. A friend convinced him to come to church that night and give God one last chance. He solemnly told God (if there even *was* a God) that he'd go to church, and that if God would reveal himself in a specific way, he might continue to believe. If not, he was done with God — and church — forever.

"God spoke to me tonight through your message," he said soberly. "That's all I needed to believe."

In Matthew 18:20, Jesus says that "where two or three gather together because they are mine, I am there among them" (NLT). When we meet together, God is present in that place. When God shows up, he reaches out to us in ways we can't anticipate. Being the church allows us to experience God's presence in a unique way.

Our Father uses his church to minister to us, to draw us

closer to him, and to equip us — these spiritual benefits aren't just for us. God is transforming his church into extraordinary ministers. He calls us to change lives in our own communities and around the world.

The Church at Its Best

Jesus said that he would build his church, and that hell could not stop it (Matt. 16:18). His words have proven true for more than twenty centuries. In parts of the world where persecution is the worst, the church seems to be at its best. Believers meet on every continent, in every kind of building, whether cathedrals, temples, theaters, barns, schools, or homes. God's church continues to grow around the world because its people instinctively understand that the church exists not for them but for those who don't yet know Christ. While the church at its best rarely makes headlines, it is changing lives — and the world — for good. It loves radically, serves sacrificially, and gives extravagantly.

Recently, one of our campuses took about forty people into the inner city to do extensive repairs on a widow's home. They figured that giving help to someone in need was a simple, straightforward way they could share their faith and demonstrate what God's love has done for them. Halfway into their workday, a couple of street-hardened teenage boys showed up and asked what was going on. One worker explained that they were fixing up this run-down house. The taller of the two boys said, "This is my grandma's house." Then both boys pitched in. It was late in the day before the boys realized these people were part of a church. Grateful for the church's help and deeply moved by how they helped their grandma, the boys agreed to come check it out. Eventually, they both committed their lives to Christ. Now they're the church, and they bring their friends to show them the church at its best.

A young man addicted to methamphetamines slipped into church, high as a kite. The message "happened" to be about overcoming addiction. He sat alone, afraid he'd be rejected for his struggles. Desperate to escape the prison of his habit, he asked a total stranger there to pray for him. That stranger "happened" to be an ex-meth user whom Christ had changed. After praying, the recovered drug addict invited his new friend to his small group Bible study. Through the support of others, that addict is now miraculously free. He is the church. Each week, he drags everyone he knows to see the church at its best.

A local church group took volunteers to a very poor apartment complex to serve its hurting people. To demonstrate the love of Christ in a practical way, dozens of church members cleaned each apartment. It was a hot summer day, about 102 degrees, and one volunteer couple stumbled onto a horrible scene. They pushed open a door to a dark and steamy room. No adults were in the apartment. Instead, they found two young babies, standing in their own feces, covered with lice and maggots. The panicked couple searched everywhere for the parents, or for anyone else who could help. Some of the other volunteers helped them clean up the children. When they still couldn't find any parents, the state took the children into protective custody. Later, the couple learned that the drug-addicted mother had abandoned her children and signed away her rights. They became foster parents and are now in the process of adopting these two children. Praise God for his church when it is at its best.

When my mom realized she was suddenly losing her eyesight, my stepdad rushed her to the emergency room. Working feverishly, a team of doctors and nurses concluded she was suffering a series of small strokes. By the time I arrived at the hospital, my mom's room was so full of people from our church that the nurses wouldn't let me in.

Over the next few days, Mom stabilized and began recovering, as the hospital struggled to manage the constant flow of people coming to support her. She was nervous about her health, but her church family constantly doted on her, loving and encouraging her.

One nurse whispered to me, "Who *are* all these people?"

I laughed. "They're from my mom's church."

She stood silent for a minute, visibly stunned. Then she said, "What church? I want to be a part of something like that."

This is the church at its best.

A couple of years ago, a single mom who danced in a local strip club visited one of our small groups. As she sat silently, trying to remain anonymous, a young man opened up about his struggles with pornography. Deeply moved both by his confession and by how the group so willingly accepted him, she decided to take a huge risk. She told them about her problem: although she had recently become a Christian, she felt trapped because she still had to strip to pay the bills. Her small group didn't pull back. Instead, they surrounded her with support and love. By the end of that meeting, they all agreed that if she'd have the faith to quit, they would help pay her bills and help her get a different job. She quit the next day. Two days later, one of the men from the group introduced her to his girlfriend, who hired her as a receptionist. Although the salary was less than she was used to, this former stripper had the unconditional support of her church family. Two years later, she *is* the church, and she helps other girls leave the stripping industry. She is the church at its best.

A Church Full of Broken People

Many Christian Atheists hesitate to join a church because they don't think there's any way God would work through them and their imperfections. But the Bible says differently. In just one example of dozens, Acts 4:13 says, "When [the religious leaders] saw the courage of Peter and John and realized that they were unschooled, ordinary men, they were astonished and they took note that these men had been with Jesus." The word we translate as "ordinary" is the Greek word *idiotes* (eed-ee-OH-tays). It means "unskilled or untrained." (You may recognize it: We derive our English word *idiot* from it.) These leaders rightly concluded that simply being with Jesus had somehow transformed Peter and John.

When Jesus called his first followers, he recruited tax collectors, uneducated fishermen, and dangerous revolutionaries. Notice who Jesus did *not* call: not one rabbi, scribe, or priest. Not one Pharisee or Sadducee, nor any other person from the formal religious establishment of the day. When he chose friends, Jesus surrounded himself with the lonely, the broken, and the overlooked. God is calling *you* to be a part of his church, to *be* his church. If you don't feel like you're good enough, then you're exactly who he's looking for. His only qualification is that you're willing to serve, like the man who answered yes:

After giving his sermon, a pastor was greeting church members in the lobby. One young man walked up to him, shook his hand, and said simply, "The answer is yes. Now what's the question?"

The pastor was visibly confused. Again the man said, "Pastor, my answer is yes. Now what's the question?"

The pastor smiled awkwardly and asked the man to explain. The man's eyes moistened, and his voice began to tremble. "Pastor, about six months ago, I was in an adulterous relationship. My life was spiraling dangerously out of control. I was at risk of losing my marriage and my family — even my job. In the middle of my storm, a mess I had made myself, you preached a message about Christ's power to change a life. It seemed like every word you preached was for me. That evening I agreed to go to a small group with my wife. I was terrified everyone would see right through me. But I was shocked when they embraced me. They invited me to meet that same Jesus you described. That night, I invited Christ to change my life — and boy, did he ever! Today my marriage and family are better than they've ever been before. God used our church to change my life."

He took a deep breath, regained his composure, and continued, "So Pastor, that's why I want you to know, my answer to you is yes. Whatever you need — anywhere, anytime — my answer is yes. Now what's the question?"

When it comes to the church, what has your answer been? Has it been no? Has it been, "Well, maybe, if I have time"? Or has it been an unconditional yes? Imagine how your life might change if you were willing to say to your church and to God, *My answer is yes. Anything. Anywhere. Anytime. Use me as your church and for your glory.*

Third Line Faith

CHARLES BLONDIN WAS A WORLD-RENOWNED TIGHTROPE artist and acrobat. On June 30, 1859, before a stunned crowd of 100,000 excited onlookers, Blondin was the first person to cross Niagara Falls by tightrope. He crossed 1100 feet on a single three-inch hemp cord, strung from 160 feet above the falls on one side to a spot 270 feet above the falls on the other. The breathless assembly watched him accomplish, step by slow step, a feat most believed impossible.

But Blondin was just getting started. In the years to come, the daring entertainer crossed again and again: on stilts, in a sack, even pushing a wheelbarrow! The story goes that an exuberant onlooker called out, "You could cross with a man in that wheelbarrow!" Blondin agreed and invited the man to climb in. The spectator nervously declined.

My dysfunctional relationship with God was often like that. I've always believed in God, just not enough to trust him with my whole life in his wheelbarrow. I knew God *could* fulfill his promises, but I was never sure he'd do it *for me*. My selfish Christian Atheist view was that God existed for me, rather than I for him. If he'd do what I thought he should, I'd trust him more. If he'd come through for me, I'd give him more of my life. If he made my life better and pain-free, I'd believe him more passionately. But anytime God didn't meet my expectations, we had a problem. God created me in his image. I returned the favor and created him in mine. The kind of God I wanted to believe in was this: if he's not what I want, then he can't have my whole life.

Whatever It Takes

Several years ago, I increasingly recognized inconsistencies between what I claimed to believe and the way I actually lived. I preached that people without Christ go to hell, but my life showed I wasn't equally passionate to reach those people. Though I believed God wanted my life to be different, I found comparing myself to others easier than measuring my life against Christ's. I preached that prayer is critical. But my prayer life was virtually nonexistent. God's Word said my treasure shouldn't be in this world, yet material things continued to grab my attention. Jesus said, "Don't worry about tomorrow." But worry came as naturally to me as breathing. If I truly belonged to Christ, I should surrender my whole life to him. I just gave him parts instead, and took them back whenever he didn't do what I wanted. I called myself a Christian, but I lived like an atheist.

The more honest I became, the more I hated living faithlessly, and the more I craved intimacy with God. "Whatever it takes" became my heart's cry. Whatever it takes to know him. Whatever it takes to live like I truly love God. Whatever it takes to love eternity more than this world. Even if I have to fight, scrape, and crawl away from my Christian Atheism into a genuine, crucified life of faith and radical obedience to Christ, I'll do whatever it takes.

Crossing the Third Line

One day I was at home working out on my elliptical machine, listening to a sermon on my iPod. Suddenly I just had to stop. Surrounded by God's presence, I knelt down on the floor and started crying out to God. If you had seen me, you would have thought I was falling apart. But God was putting me back together.

I cried for all of God, and his presence became immediately real. Although I'd unquestionably been spiritually reborn a decade and a half ago, it was like I was being born again — again.

I've always believed in spiritual visions; I'd just never had one. Not anymore. I saw a picture as clear as the words on this page. I stood before three lines in the sand. Somehow I knew what each line represented.

Line 1: I believe in God and the gospel of Christ enough to benefit from it. Like so many others, crossing that first line was easy. Sadly, many who call themselves Christians live here. If there *is* a God, I want to be on his good side. I want to go to heaven. I want him to bless me with good health, good relationships, and a happy life. Like the nine ungrateful lepers in Luke 17, once God had helped me, I forgot about him.

Most wouldn't admit that this is all the faith they can manage. We want God's benefits without changing how we live. We want his best, without our sacrifices. At the first line, we don't fear God or share our faith. We still love this world. We'll pursue happiness at any cost. The list goes on and on. We first-line believers get what we can from God without giving much, if anything, back.

Is first-line faith *real* Christianity? Is believing in Jesus enough? Although God is the only true judge, I'm not sure that simply believing in Christ makes a person a Christian. Honestly, I'm tempted to say, "No, I sincerely don't think it is real Christianity." Even demons believe in Christ. I worry how many people might be deceived. Instead of truly living as followers of Christ, many lull themselves into a sense of false comfort. What if they're really "cultural Christians," false believers? I don't point my finger at others, only at myself. For way too long, I've claimed a belief in God, but my life didn't reflect it.

Line 2: I believe in God and Christ's gospel enough to contribute comfortably. Past the first line are people who believe in God not only enough to benefit but also enough to give back — as long as it doesn't cost too much. Many first-line Christians eventually cross the second line. *If I don't have to change too much, I'll do some of what God asks. If it doesn't hurt too much, I'll get more serious about God. But everyone has their limits, right?* Like the rich young ruler in Matthew 19, I was willing to go along with the religious rules as long as it didn't hurt too much.

There, on the floor next to my elliptical, still crying, I realized: *I* was a second-line believer. I'd serve Jesus in ministry, but I didn't want too many critics. I'd give up some things for Christ, but being away from my family often was too much. I'd follow Jesus anywhere — as long as the job included insurance for my family. The third line was just inches in front of me.

It might as well have been miles.

Line 3: I believe in God and Christ's gospel enough to give my life to it. Although most people I knew were line-one and line-two believers, suddenly anything less than line three didn't seem like real Christianity to me. Could I give my whole life to Christ? Not only in words but in my daily life?

Verses I'd read dozens of times suddenly flooded to mind:

"For whoever wants to save his life will lose it, but whoever loses his life for me will find it. What good will it be for a man if he gains the whole world, yet forfeits his soul?" (Matt. 16:25 – 26). Am I willing to lose my life?

"I have been crucified with Christ and I no longer live, but Christ lives in me. The life I live in the body, I live by faith in the Son of God, who loved me and gave himself for me" (Gal. 2:20). Could I sacrifice my desires, my hopes, my dreams?

"However, I consider my life worth nothing to me, if only I may finish the race and complete the task the Lord Jesus has given me — the task of testifying to the gospel" (Acts 20:24). What would it take to make my life nothing to me, existing only to do what Christ wants me to?

"What is more, I consider everything a loss compared to the surpassing greatness of knowing Christ Jesus my Lord, for whose sake I have lost all things. I consider them rubbish, that I may gain Christ" (Phil. 3:8). Could I truly count all my earthly possessions a loss, making Christ my greatest treasure?

Christ or Nothing

I knew in the deepest part of myself: I have to be a third-line believer. With unquenchable thirst, I pursued living water above all substitutes. I started praying like never before. I started pursuing God in the morning and continued throughout the day. Jesus was on my mind when I fell asleep and when I awoke. Scripture started becoming my bread of life, nourishing my soul.

I surrendered one thing after another, until just one major hurdle stood between where I was and where God wanted me. I can't tell you what that thing was. It's simply too personal. Only two people in the world know it.

My battle to cross the third line lasted almost two years. I prayed about it daily. I quoted Scripture. Though spiritually exhausted, I wouldn't give up. Spiritual warfare raged around me. Finally, on one very normal Saturday afternoon, by faith, I gave this last part of my life totally to God. I sacrificed a fear that had held me hostage since I was a child and made a promise to God that I'd never take it back.

I crossed the third line.

I believe in God and Christ's gospel so much that I'm willing to give my whole life to his cause. Nothing in this world is more important to me than my treasure in heaven. No fear in my heart is greater than my fear of God. I desire nothing more than I desire all of God. Tears are filling my eyes as I type this. I cannot put into words what God has done in my heart.

I am a different person.

You can be too.

Don't forget, the world will try to pull us back across the third line, the second line, and even across the first line. But we won't retreat or back down. Every day, we'll choose to live out our belief in God instead of believing in the world or ourselves. When we truly *know* God, rather than living ashamed of our past of doubting God's love for us, we can daily enjoy his grace and unconditional love and acceptance. As our faith and prayer life grows, we'll see his goodness — even in our trials — and grow to forgive as he has freely forgiven us. Instead of believing we can never change, we can let his unlimited power transform us and lead us out of a life paralyzed by fear and worry. Because God isn't just someone we believe in but is our life, we won't seek security and happiness in the things of the world but will find them in his presence and will. As he consumes us, strengthened by his church, we'll seize opportunities to share his love with people daily. The choice is ours.

Every day I choose the third line.

Your Turn

Are you a Christian Atheist? Do you believe in God but live as if he doesn't exist? I am praying that God leads you beyond first-line faith. Believing in Christ enough to benefit from him is at best shallow Christianity. At worst, it's empty, deceptive religion, leading many down the broad path to eternal devastation.

Step across the first line — but don't stop there.

Line two will feel much better than line one. Believing in Christ enough to contribute comfortably may seem right. But even that is a human-centered Christianity. Keep moving.

Consider the third line. Ask what separates you from a wholly surrendered, Spirit-filled, kingdom-driven life. Weigh your options. Life as it is … or life as it could be.

Consider the costs.

Do whatever it takes.

Step across the line.

Welcome to true Christianity.

Acknowledgments

To everyone who contributed to *The Christian Atheist*,
I'm very grateful.

I'm especially indebted to:

Dudley Delffs, Angela Scheff, Tom Dean, Brian Phipps,
and the whole team at Zondervan — it is an honor to
partner with you.

Tom Winters — thanks for believing in this project long
before anyone else did.

Brannon Golden and Brian Smith — you are amazing with
words.

Ali Bergin, Lori Bailey, Bongi Wenyika, and Sarah
McLean — thanks for reading the manuscript and offering
your valuable suggestions.

Catie, Mandy, Anna, Sam, Bookie, and Joy — there is no
dad in the world more blessed than I am.

Amy — you are the best Christian I know. Let's grow old
together.

it

How Churches and Leaders Can Get It and Keep It

Craig Groeschel

When Craig Groeschel founded Life Church.tv, the congregation met in a borrowed two-car garage with ratty furnishings and faulty audiovisual equipment. But people were drawn there, sensing a powerful, life-changing force Groeschel calls *it*.

What is *it*, and how can you and your ministry get—and keep—*it*? Combining in-your-face honesty with off-the-wall humor, this book tells how any believer can obtain *it*, get *it* back, and guard *it*.

One of today's most innovative church leaders, Groeschel provides profile interviews with Mark Driscoll, Perry Noble, Tim Stevens, Mark Batterson, Jud Wilhite, and Dino Rizzo.

This lively book will challenge churches and their leaders to maintain the spiritual balance that results in experiencing *it* in their lives.

Hardcover, Jacketed Printed: 978-0-310-28682-0
Audio Download, Unabridged: 978-0-310-30244-5

Pick up a copy at your favorite bookstore or online!

it

How Churches and Leaders Can Get It and Keep It

Craig Groeschel

Craig Groeschel, founding and senior pastor of LifeChurch.tv, takes you on a nine-session video journey to discover the powerful presence from God that he calls *it* at work in many churches. Each video session is approximately ten-minutes long and focuses on the many facets of what *it* is and where *it* comes from. Craig explores the necessary contributions to *it*, such as vision, divine focus, unmistakable camaraderie, innovative minds, willingness to fall short, hearts focused outward, and kingdom-mindedness. He concludes the video experience with a session on whether you have *it* and how to keep *it* once you have *it*. This video is designed for leadership groups and church groups and includes discussion questions on the DVD at the end of each session.

DVD: 978-0-310-94213-9

Pick up a copy at your favorite bookstore or online!